just add water

also by lauren chattman

Cool Kitchen

william morrow and company, inc.

New York

just add water

Can You Boil Water? Then you can make 140 Deliciously Simple Recipes for Great Soups, Stews, Chicken, Fish, Pasta, Desserts, and More

lauren chattman

It is the policy of William Morrow and Company, Inc.,
and its imprints and affiliates, recognizing the importance of
preserving what has been written, to print the books we publish on
acid-free paper, and we exert our best efforts to that end.

Library of Congress Cataloging-in-Publication Data

Chattman, Lauren.
    Just add water : can you boil water? Then you can
make 140 deliciously simple recipes for great soups,
stews, chicken, fish, pasta, desserts, and more / by Lauren
Chattman. — 1st ed.
        p.   cm.
    Includes index.
    ISBN 0-688-16188-X
    1. Boiling (Cookery)   I. Title.
TX685.C48   1999
641.7'3—dc21   98-8295
                                                        CIP

Printed in the United States of America

First Edition

1 2 3 4 5 6 7 8 9 10

BOOK DESIGN BY MARYSARAH QUINN

www.williammorrow.com

For my parents,
authorities on food and fun

Contents

acknowledgments

Angela Miller helped with this project from beginning to end.

I am privileged to have worked with Pam Hoenig again. Her support for all of my quick-cook ideas, however crazy they might have sounded at first, means so much to me.

I'm grateful for the wonderful work Naomi Glikman, Carrie Weinberg, Corinne Alhadeff, Claire Israel, and Marysarah Quinn have done on my behalf.

Thanks to Harry Fischman for designing a beautiful new kitchen for us. Thanks to Andrea Ackerman and Alexandra Fischman for sampling my experimental boiled dinners.

My sisters, Barri and Stacey, offered their own encouragement when they both said that a book like this might actually get them to cook.

Special thanks to Jack Bishop for letting me take over the new kitchen and to my daughter, Rose, who prefers boiled food over any other kind.

And thanks to my parents, Marty and Marilyn Chattman, whose love of food and fun inspires everyone who shares a meal with them.

the boiled and the beautiful

effortless cooking

For several years now, I have attempted to make great food with as little labor as possible. The first product of this effort, if you can call it that, was *Cool Kitchen,* a book of recipes that actually require no cooking at all. After gratefully accepting a copy, one of my friends, an enthusiastic eater but inexperienced cook, remarked, "Now I could use a book on how to boil water." The wheels started turning, and *Just Add Water* is the result.

At the time, I was working on a magazine article about quick-cooking grains. I had recipes for bulgur, polenta, and couscous, all of which are quickly rehydrated with boiling water before being combined with a few flavorful ingredients and served in minutes flat.

Digging into a bulgur and smoked chicken salad dressed with cumin, olive oil, and lemon juice and sprinkled with pine nuts and fresh herbs, I wondered how many other great dinners I could come up with if I limited myself to boiling water.

It began as a kind of game, but after my list grew to include some of my favorite pastas, soups, stews, and desserts, I realized the appeal of this food. Pearl Barley, Porcini, and Parmesan; Beef Short Ribs with Exotic Spices; Warm Chocolate-Espresso Pudding—each of these dishes requires little effort and is deeply satisfying. Just the kind of food I like to cook and eat for dinner every night.

When I started my list, I didn't consider myself a big fan of boiling. I like big flavors and food I can sink my teeth into. Like most people, I equated boiling with bland food that's been cooked to mush. But once I thought about the technique more carefully, I realized that this is a misconception. There are ways to use boiling so that it brings out the flavors of food. Boiling allows curry, coconut, and carrots to blend in an exciting and delicious way in Curried Cream of Carrot Soup. Simply boiled vegetables are a wonderful canvas for a variety of exuberant dressings; think about Blanched Asparagus with Olive Oil and Manchego or Broccoli Rabe with Garlic-Chile Oil. As for texture, boiling can work wonders on certain foods, rendering dried beans creamy and transforming granulated sugar and nuts into amber-colored praline candy. When a tough pork roast is cooked with rock-hard yams, not only do the ingredients benefit from each other's flavors but they also become meltingly tender.

I must have known all of this instinctively, even if I hadn't yet acknowledged the centrality of boiling in my everyday cooking. Well before I conceived of this book, I often gravitated toward dishes with bold flavors that require little more than filling a pot and lighting a burner. Black Bean Soup with a Shot of Scotch is an old favorite that fits the bill. For years I've been making a creamy Arborio Rice Pudding that never fails to satisfy. I suspect that a lot of people, novices and accomplished cooks alike, want the same thing—recipes with style and integrity that also just happen to be so easy that even a cooking idiot can make them. Boiling is the answer.

When you open this book, feel confident that there will be no unfamiliar or tricky steps like browning, broiling, baking, or barbecuing lurking within the recipes. There's just a single cooking method—boiling—uniting each and every one. If you are sipping drip coffee or nibbling on steamed broccoli while you read this, you are ready to cook.

boiling for everyone

Boiling is easy. Anyone who's ever lived with a hot plate can boil water. Even people who have never baked cookies, sautéed onions, or scrambled eggs can make a cup of tea. You can't spoil a boiled dinner by burning it; there's no possibility of a grease fire. Why not use this underrated and easily mastered technique to create delicious everyday meals? If your sophistication about food outstrips your kitchen know-how, you'll appreciate *Just Add Water*'s imaginative recipes and practical approach. Even if your knowledge extends beyond boiling, you'll be delighted with the streamlined food in the chapters that follow.

Just Add Water provides ideas for every meal and occasion.

Great breakfasts don't have to involve yeast-raised waffles or perfectly executed omelets. Instead of an uninviting bowl of cold corn flakes, how about Grits and Goat Cheese or Oatmeal with Almonds and Grated Apples?

Boiled vegetables might not sound terribly sexy, but in fact boiling is one of the quickest, most healthful ways to prepare an amazing variety of side dishes and salads. Blanched Leeks with Ricotta Salata Vinaigrette are the opposite of bland. The same goes for New Potatoes with Lemon-Dill Pesto. Both are fresh and lively, and both are boiled.

Soup making doesn't have to involve difficult and time-consuming stocks or the messy sautéing of meat and vegetables. Many special soups require little more than tossing a few ingredients into a large pot of water. My Italian Tomato and Bread Soup is wonderful "peasant" food, rustic and filling. The secret? Simmered tomatoes, garlic, and olive oil ladled over chunks of chewy country bread. Saffron Mussel Bisque is more refined, but just as basic to make: Steam some mussels, enrich the resulting broth with cream, season with a few precious threads of saffron and a spoonful of chopped fresh chives, and serve.

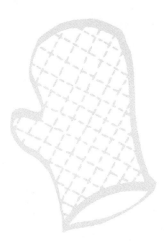

Aside from being nutritious and cheap, boiled beans are simple to prepare and versatile beyond belief. Either combine boiled beans with flavorful dressings, like the Kidney Beans with Walnut Dressing, or boil them along with flavoring ingredients for heartier stews like Black Beans Boiled in Beer.

Pasta has long been a standby of the "how to boil water" crowd, but there are many other grain dishes well within reach. Like pasta, rice can be boiled and sauced in a million different ways. Try Boiled Arborio Rice with Smoked Salmon and Capers if you're looking for a luxurious but simple alternative to pasta. Flavorful grain salads like Bulgur and Carrots with Cumin-Coriander Dressing provide

color and interest alongside simple grilled or broiled fish and chicken.

It's easy enough to make Cod Fillets in Fennel Broth once you know that "poaching" is a fancy word for boiling. If roasting and grilling are not in your repertoire, that doesn't mean you have to live without soul-satisfying meat dishes. My Hearty Beef Stew requires no browning—just "simmering" (another fancy word for boiling) in wine and water.

To finish, there are wonderful no-bake desserts. Rum-Vanilla Panna Cotta is an elevated Jell-O dessert (your friends don't have to know this) made with cream, dark rum, a vanilla bean, and unflavored gelatin. Crave something sweet and light that comes from the farmstand rather than a bright green box? Let Peaches in Rosemary–Red Wine Syrup deliver you from SnackWell hell.

A list of menus at the end of the book will give you some ideas about how to put together simple but satisfying meals for family and friends. You know all those people you owe dinner invitations? You'll feel entirely capable of reciprocating once you see how easy it is to make a complete meal when you just add water.

how to boil water

If you already feel comfortable boiling water, skip right to the recipes in the following chapters. If you are a boiling neophyte, read on for simple explanations and model recipes illustrating boiling in its various guises.

simple boiling

No less an eminence than James Beard began his book *Theory and Practice of Good Cooking* with a chapter on boiling and its applications. Whether your kitchen ambitions are basic or grand, you need to know how to boil. If you don't, you can't make poached eggs or pasta. Neither can you make veal stock or a soufflé.

Whenever you cook food in hot, bubbling liquid, whether it's pasta in salted water, stew meat in red wine, or pears in sugar syrup, you are boiling. Simple boiling, or what's also called a hard or full boil during which the liquid maintains a temperature of 212 degrees, requires very little monitoring or finesse. When boiling pasta, rice, or vegetables, fill your pot with water, turn the heat to high, and bring the water to a rolling boil. Toss in a little salt and the food you want to cook, and drain when tender but not mushy.

Be sure to fill your pot with enough water to cook whatever you are cooking, but not so much that it will boil over. You salt the water to give your food a little bit of flavor. One tablespoon per pound of pasta might seem like a lot, but remember that most of the salt will go right down the drain with the water. One pound of pasta should be cooked in 4 quarts of boiling water. One cup of rice requires 3 quarts of water and 1 tablespoon salt. Use a pot that can hold twice as much water as you are using to allow room for bubbling. Always leave the pan uncovered to prevent overboiling.

perfect white rice

Rice cooked *in abundant salted water produces fluffy grains with a pleasant starchiness, good for soaking up the juices of a stew. Boiled rice has the advantage in cleanup, too, since there's no difficult-to-remove crust left at the bottom of the pan.*

3 quarts water

I tablespoon salt

I cup long-grain white rice

I. Bring the water to boil in a large saucepan. Add the salt and then slowly pour in the rice. Boil until tender but not mushy, about 15 minutes.

2. Drain rice well in a colander, fluff with a fork, and serve immediately.

makes 4 servings

simmering

Simmering is a gentle form of boiling, protecting delicate foods from the violent rolling action of a hard boil and giving tough foods time to soften up. When a pot of liquid is brought to a full boil, bubbles continually emerge and completely cover the surface. When a pot of liquid is simmered, there might be several spots on the surface that release bubbles, but most of the surface is calm.

Grains are often simmered, allowing them to absorb liquid evenly before the bottom layer has time to dry out and stick to the pan. If cooked in rapidly boiling water, beans tend to lose their skins and begin to break apart before they are fully cooked. So instead, they should be gently simmered until tender. Simmering is essential for many kinds of soups, allowing the ingredients to release their flavors more slowly into the pot. Tough cuts of meat are tenderized when exposed to gentle, moist heat.

Simmering requires a little more attention than simple boiling. You have to check the pot periodically to make sure that bubbles are occasionally breaking the surface. If your pot is boiling rapidly enough so that the surface is visible only as a mass of bubbles, turn the heat down; if nothing is happening, turn the heat up a little. Check your pot periodically to make sure you are not under- or overboiling your food.

chicken stock

Stocks and soups *are slowly simmered to give ingredients time to release their flavors. I like to simmer my chicken stock for a good three hours. I use dill because it's what my mother's always used, but you may substitute a bunch of parsley for a more neutral flavor, if you like. Freeze chicken stock in 1- and 2-cup portions so you can thaw it out a little bit at a time when you need it.*

4 pounds chicken backs, wings, and/or whole legs

3½ quarts water

1 medium-size onion, peeled and cut into medium-size dice

1 large bunch fresh dill

2 bay leaves

2 teaspoons salt

1. Place the chicken and water in a large stockpot or soup kettle. Bring to a boil, reduce the heat to medium or medium-low, and simmer, uncovered, for 7 minutes, using a mesh skimmer to remove any foam that rises to the surface. Add the onion, dill, bay leaves, and salt and simmer for another 3 hours.

2. Strain the broth through a fine sieve; discard the bones. Skim the fat using a gravy skimmer, or refrigerate overnight and skim off the solidified fat with a spoon. Refrigerate for up to 3 days or freeze for up to 3 months.

makes about **8 cups**

poaching

Poached food is completely immersed in simmering or almost-simmering liquid. It is either cooked over a very low heat or removed from the heat and allowed to stand in the hot liquid until cooked. Poached food stays wonderfully moist because it is always covered in water and cooked so gently. Poached chicken breasts and salmon fillets can be used to create innumerable salads and main dishes. For poaching fruit, see page 230.

perfect poached chicken breasts

I like to *poach chicken breasts in a flavorful broth, but you can also use plain water. The important thing is never to let the liquid come to a real boil; you just want an occasional bubble to break the surface. Finishing the chicken by removing it from the heat and letting it stand in the poaching liquid ensures cooked but not overcooked breasts.*

3 cups homemade chicken stock (page 8) or canned low-sodium chicken broth

¾ cup dry white wine

1 garlic clove, peeled and crushed

1½ teaspoons salt

2 whole boneless, skinless chicken breasts, split

1. In a large saucepan, bring the stock, wine, garlic, and salt to a boil. Reduce the heat to a simmer and add the chicken breasts. Cover and cook at a bare simmer for 5 minutes. Turn the chicken, cover, and cook for another 5 minutes.

2. Remove the skillet from the heat, uncover, and let the chicken stand in the poaching liquid for 30 minutes. Check to ensure the chicken is cooked all the way through. Refrigerate until ready to use, up to 2 days.

makes 4 servings

perfect poached salmon

Salmon *has such a delicate texture that even gently simmering water can cause little bits of it to flake off. I like to place it in water that's been brought to a boil and then remove the pot from the heat, allowing it to finish cooking as the water cools.*

4 salmon fillets, about 6 ounces each

1. Fill a large saucepan with enough water to cover the fillets. Bring the water to a boil. With a wide spatula, carefully place the fish in the pan, cover, and turn off the heat. Let the fish sit in the water for 30 minutes.

2. Carefully remove the fish from the water, again with the wide spatula. It should flake all the way through. Transfer to a serving platter and serve, or refrigerate up to 2 days and serve chilled.

makes 4 servings

steaming

Food can be cooked in the steam produced by boiling water (or another liquid like juice, beer, or wine) rather than the boiling water itself. Food that is steamed retains its natural juices and is kept moist by the circulating vapors.

Frankly, I think boiled vegetables, if well cooked and well drained, are just as good in simple salads as steamed ones. But if you're cooking vegetables and then serving them plain or as part of a crudité platter, you might consider steaming, since there's less of a chance of overcooking and no chance that they will be soggy.

To steam vegetables, place a collapsible steamer basket or a steamer insert into a saucepan containing a little bit of water. The bottom of the steamer should stand about 1 inch above the water, so that the food won't come into direct contact with the water even when it is boiling. Place the vegetables in the basket. Cover and bring to a boil. Steam until the vegetables are tender but not mushy. Small pieces and tender vegetables (green beans, peas, cauliflower, asparagus, broccoli) will cook in less than 5 minutes from the time the water comes to a boil. Larger pieces and tougher vegetables will take longer—you'll need to check on them.

Clams, mussels, lobster, and crab can also be steamed. Steaming keeps shellfish moist but doesn't make them waterlogged. In the case of clams and mussels, a little bit of wine or water in the pot combines with the juices released as the shells open, producing a flavorful broth. Shellfish can be placed directly into the pot with the water—no need for a steamer basket.

steamers

Steamers *are soft-shell clams that make a flavorful broth when cooked in a little water. Since they can be quite sandy even when thoroughly washed, the broth they give off can be used to "rinse" them before dipping in melted butter.*

6 pounds steamer clams

½ pound unsalted butter, melted and
    kept hot

1. Rinse the steamers by placing them in a large bowl, filling it with cold water, and draining. Do this several times until the water looks clear. Discard any broken steamers or steamers that will not close.

2. Put 1 inch of water in a large stockpot. Place the steamers in the pot. Cover, turn the heat to high, and cook, stirring once or twice, until the steamers have all opened, 7 to 10 minutes. Remove the steamers with a slotted spoon and place in a large serving bowl. Discard any that will not open.

3. Pour the broth through a colander lined with cheesecloth or paper towels. Serve the steamers with individual bowls of hot broth and butter for dipping.

makes 4 servings

reducing

Reducing means boiling down a liquid to thicken it and concentrate its flavor. The liquid in which stew meat is cooked is sometimes reduced to make an intense sauce. Before reducing stew juices, remove the meat with a slotted spoon. (Cooking the tender chunks in rapidly boiling liquid might make them fall apart.) Then turn the heat to high and boil the juices down until they are slightly thick-ened. Return the meat to the pot to heat through.

Dessert sauces are often made by reducing fruit juice or fortified wine. Because these sauces are made in relatively small quantities, they reduced quickly. Watch sweet sauces carefully and remove them from the heat when reduced and slightly thickened but before so much liquid has evaporated that the sugar begins to burn.

apple cider syrup

Here's a simple alternative *to maple syrup—a little apple cider that's sweetened with honey, reduced, and enriched with butter. Serve over pancakes, waffles, or French toast.*

I cup apple cider

I tablespoon honey

I tablespoon fresh lemon juice

I tablespoon unsalted butter

1. Combine the cider, honey, and lemon juice in a small saucepan. Bring to a boil, reduce the heat to a lively simmer, and cook until the mixture is reduced by half (judge this by eye, or pour the mixture into a glass measuring cup and return to the pan if it hasn't reduced enough).

2. Remove pan from the heat and stir in the butter. Serve warm or refrigerate for up to a week and reheat (but do not boil, or the butter will separate from the syrup) before serving.

makes ½ cup, enough to top 2 servings of pancakes

using a double boiler

Some ingredients are so delicate that it's best to cook them in a double boiler to shield them from direct heat. Egg-based sauces like hollandaise will become lumpy if not cooked this way. Chocolate should be slowly melted in a double boiler to prevent separation and graininess.

A double boiler is a pot within a pot. The bottom pot holds a small amount of water, no more than 1 inch to prevent overboiling. The top pot holds whatever ingredients you'll be heating and fits snugly inside the bottom. If you don't own a double boiler, you can easily improvise one by filling a saucepan with no more than 1 inch of water, bringing it to the barest simmer, and placing a heatproof bowl on top of the pan. Make sure that the bowl does not touch the water so that your ingredients don't become hot too quickly. Peek into the bottom pot periodically to make sure the water doesn't come to a full boil.

white chocolate sauce

White chocolate *is even more unstable than dark, so it requires extra care in heating and handling. A saucepan of hot but not quite simmering water underneath a heatproof glass bowl will melt the chocolate without overheating it and turning it grainy. Serve this sauce over fudgy brownies still warm from the oven, or use as a dip for ripe strawberries.*

6 ounces white chocolate

4 tablespoons (½ stick) unsalted butter, cut into several pieces

¼ cup heavy cream

1. Place 1 inch of water in a large saucepan and place over the lowest heat. Combine the chocolate, butter, and heavy cream in a heatproof bowl large enough to sit on top of the pan. Place the bowl over the hot water, making sure that the bottom of the bowl does not touch the water. Check the water temperature periodically by lifting the bowl with an oven mitt. If the water begins to steam at all, turn the heat off and let the chocolate melt from the residual heat in the pot. Let the bowl stand over the water until the chocolate is melted, whisking often, 7 to 10 minutes.

2. Remove bowl from the heat and whisk sauce until smooth. Serve immediately, or refrigerate up to 1 week and reheat over warm water again.

makes about 1 cup, enough to serve 4 as a dip

essential equipment for boiling

If you're only going to boil, you don't need a professionally equipped or even a well-equipped kitchen. A few pots and pans, a colander, and a wooden spoon will probably do. If you've ever cooked anything at all, your kitchen is probably adequately equipped for any of the recipes in this book, but just in case you don't know what a whisk is, don't panic. Here is a list of equipment useful if you're just going to add water.

Blender: A blender is an especially useful appliance for making vegetable purees and pureed soups. A fancy blender with settings for everything from stirring, grating, and crushing ice is nice but not necessary. A basic model with an on-off button is fine for any of the recipes in this book.

Colander: If you are going to cook food in boiling water, you are probably going to have to drain it. Colanders are inexpensive and indispensable. I have a set of three, in different sizes, for draining everything from 2 pounds of pasta to one diced potato.

Double boiler: A pot within a pot, used to warm foods over indirect heat. It is not neces-

sary to buy a double boiler, since you can easily improvise one by placing a heatproof bowl over a saucepan filled with an inch of simmering water. Use a double boiler to melt chocolate, make mousses, and keep mashed potatoes warm without drying them out.

Food processor: Although a food processor might seem like an expensive item to own if you don't know a lot about cooking, it is actually extraordinarily useful for a beginning cook. I use mine to make everything from pesto to pizza dough. You can get along without one, but if you are really interested in saving time in the kitchen, you won't want to.

Gravy skimmer: This is a useful gadget for separating and discarding the fat from gravies, stocks, and soups. It looks like a measuring cup, but the spout draws liquid from the bottom of the cup; the fat rises to the top. When you pour from the cup, you pour the gravy or stock and leave the fat behind. Skimmed stock or gravy is not only healthier but also tastes better because it is less greasy.

Measuring cups and spoons: For best results with these recipes, measure precisely. Liquids should be poured into clear "liquid" measuring cups, which resemble little pitchers and have lines drawn on the outside for easy reading. I use glass Pyrex cups because they won't crack or melt on contact with boiling liquid. For grains, beans, and other dry ingredients, use plastic or metal "dry" measuring cups and spoons. Fill the cups and spoons completely and level off with a knife for precise measurements.

Mesh skimmer: This long-handled implement is useful in skimming foam, which contains off-tasting impurities, from the surface of simmering stock.

Saucepan: A saucepan is a basic pot with deep sides, essential for boiling. It is helpful to have a variety of sizes, from 8 quarts (which can accommodate a pound of pasta) to 1 quart or smaller, for reducing dessert sauces, heating small quantities of soup or stock, or melting butter. Avoid lightweight aluminum pans, since they tend to scorch foods. Choose heavier "anodized" aluminum or stainless steel. Sometimes you'll need covers for your saucepans and sometimes you won't.

Sieve: A sieve is necessary for straining stocks and sauces. When you make chicken stock, for example, you want to end up with a clear broth. So you pour the contents of your stockpot through a sieve to strain out the bits of chicken and herbs that have been cooked to flavor the broth. In a pinch, you can use a colander lined with paper towels instead of a sieve.

Slotted spoon: A useful tool for lifting chunks of food out of boiling or simmering liquid.

Steamer basket: Either a collapsible aluminum basket or a steamer insert made especially for a saucepan. Use the steamer basket to cook vegetables.

Stockpot: A large pot, at least 10 quarts. Use a stockpot for boiling large quantities of liquid, as when making stock. Or use it when steaming shellfish, which take up a lot of room.

Wire whisk: A wire whisk is great for breaking up lumps in whatever you are heating. Use it for melting chocolate, dissolving gelatin, stirring cornmeal into boiling water for polenta, and any other recipe where you don't want any lumps in the finished product.

Wooden spoon: Metal can get very hot and plastic can melt. When boiling, use a wooden spoon rather than metal or plastic for stirring.

boil yourself

some breakfast

Hot Ginger Lemonade

◆

French Roast Coffee with Chocolate Cream

◆

Peppermint Hot Chocolate

◆

Oatmeal with Almonds and Grated Apples

◆

Grits and Goat Cheese

◆

Pumpkin Polenta

◆

Honey-Date Breakfast Couscous

◆

Homemade Applesauce

◆

Egg and Avocado Salad with Spicy Red Salsa on the Side

◆

Spinach Salad with Ham and Poached Eggs

◆

Dried Fruit Compote

You've finally mastered the art of making coffee. You've got your stylish French press coffeepot, your cutting-edge frothing device, your turbinado sugar. But instead of feeling empowered, you are a little bit embarrassed. "This is not breakfast. What would my mother say?" Somehow pouring a bowl of corn flakes to go along with your perfect latte doesn't really make you feel better.

Breakfast is a natural starting point for people who know how to boil water but don't feel competent doing anything else. Cast aside any feelings of anxiety or defeat. Great breakfasts don't have to involve yeast-raised waffles or perfectly executed omelets. This chapter will show you how to use the skill you already have to make warming, wonderful breakfast dishes.

Build on your coffee-making experience by expanding your hot beverage repertoire. Hot Ginger Lemonade and French Roast Coffee with Chocolate Cream may require one or two more ingredients than coffee, but are well within the reach of any beginning water boiler. I have only one helpful hint here: if you're heating milk, watch it carefully so that

it just comes to a boil and doesn't boil over. This has happened to me more times than I can say. Cleaning up the mess around one of my burners always decreases (but certainly never wipes out) the pleasure I take in a steaming mug of Peppermint Hot Chocolate.

It's only a baby step from hot chocolate to hot cereal. The down-home sophistication of Grits and Goat Cheese is sure to please your usual brunch dates as well as your mom, and requires nothing in the way of skill aside from bringing water to a boil. A little chopping, a little mixing, and you get Oatmeal with Almonds and Grated Apples. Making great hot cereal is the opposite of tricky. Do make sure to turn the heat very low once you add your cornmeal or oatmeal. As it thickens, boiling polenta and oats take on the molten characteristics of lava, erupting in large bubbles that might burst and burn your stirring hand. There's no such danger with breakfast couscous, since you turn the heat off as soon as your water comes to a boil.

I've included two simple fruit preparations for the times when you want something a little more elaborate than a glass of orange juice or half a grapefruit. Homemade Applesauce, that staple of kindergarten cookery, is one of the simplest and best comfort foods I know. Dried Fruit Compote, flavored with vanilla and star anise, is a notch above applesauce in flavor complexity, but might easily be prepared by kindergarten cooks. Eat either one on its own, or serve over French toast or pancakes, if you dare.

Eggs, the elemental breakfast food, are made for boiling. The recipes in this chapter contain foolproof directions for hard-cooking and poaching. Speaking from experience, I urge you to remove your hard-cooked eggs from the heat as soon as the water comes to a boil and let them finish cooking by standing, covered, in the hot water. If you forgetfully let the water evaporate from the pan you might be left with a mess of exploded eggs accompanied by a very unpleasant burning smell.

Poaching eggs is as simple as hard-cooking. It just takes a gentle touch, a kitchen timer, and a slotted spoon to ensure unbroken, perfectly cooked yolks.

hot ginger lemonade

Hot ginger lemonade *is great for soothing a cold, or just chasing away a winter chill. I like the distinctive taste of honey, but sugar can be substituted if you like.*

2 tablespoons fresh lemon juice

2 tablespoons honey, or more to taste

One 1-inch piece fresh gingerroot, peeled
    and sliced into 4 pieces

2 cups water

1. Combine all the ingredients in a medium-size saucepan and bring to a boil. Remove the ginger and discard.

2. Pour into two mugs and serve immediately.

makes 2 servings

french roast coffee with chocolate cream

Maybe I should have *called this Chocolate Cream with French Roast Coffee instead of the other way around, since it resembles rich hot cocoa. In any case, fans of coffee–chocolate combinations will happily begin a weekend morning with this brew.*

3 cups milk or half-and-half

4 ounces semisweet chocolate, finely chopped

½ teaspoon pure vanilla extract

1 cup hot, fresh-brewed French roast coffee or espresso

1. Heat the milk or half-and-half in a small saucepan over medium-high heat. When it just comes to a boil, remove from the heat and whisk in the chocolate. Continue whisking until all the chocolate has melted and the mixture is frothy. Stir in the vanilla.

2. Pour the coffee into four large mugs. Pour the chocolate cream over the coffee. Serve immediately.

makes 4 servings

peppermint hot chocolate

Other extracts *can be substituted for the peppermint—almond or hazelnut,*
for example—to make exquisitely flavored hot chocolate. For extra richness, substitute
1 cup heavy cream for 1 cup of the milk.

4 cups milk

6 ounces semisweet chocolate,
   finely chopped

1 tablespoon unsweetened cocoa powder

½ teaspoon pure peppermint extract

1. Bring just to a boil over medium-high heat. Reduce the heat to low and whisk in the chocolate and cocoa powder. Continue to whisk until all the chocolate is melted and the mixture is smooth.

2. Remove the pan from the heat and stir in the peppermint extract. Pour the hot chocolate into mugs and serve immediately.

makes 4 servings

oatmeal with almonds and grated apples

Using a grated *rather than a chopped apple gives this oatmeal great texture without making it too chunky. I like tart apples like Granny Smith or McIntosh, but choose your favorite. Pears also work well here.*

3½ cups water

¼ teaspoon salt

2 cups old-fashioned rolled oats (not instant)

1 large apple, cored, peeled, and coarsely grated

¼ cup firmly packed brown sugar, or more to taste

¼ teaspoon ground cinnamon

Pinch of ground nutmeg

¼ cup sliced almonds

Unsalted butter and/or milk or heavy cream (optional)

1. Bring the water and salt to boil in a medium-size saucepan. Stir in the oats, reduce the heat to a bare simmer, and cook, stirring frequently, until most of the water is absorbed, about 5 minutes. Stir in the apple, brown sugar, cinnamon, and nutmeg.

2. Divide the oatmeal among four bowls. Scatter some of the almonds on top of each portion. Serve with butter and/or milk or cream on the side if desired.

makes 4 servings

expand your cereal horizons

1. **Experiment with sweeteners.** Try cinnamon sugar, maple syrup, honey, molasses, chunky fruit jams, Hershey's chocolate syrup (just kidding—but dusting a bowl of sweetened oatmeal with cocoa powder might not be too bad).

2. **Try Irish oatmeal.** This variety takes longer to cook, 30 to 45 minutes, but has great heft and whole-grain flavor that more heavily processed oats have lost.

3. **Oatmeal is great, but so are other hot cereals.** Revisit cream of wheat or cream of rice. Check out your health food store: Bulgur, barley, wheat berries, and other good grains all become breakfast if you just add water.

4. **Beyond boiling:** Make your own granola. Preheat the oven to 325 degrees. Mix 4 cups of old-fashioned rolled oats (not instant), 2 teaspoons ground cinnamon, 1½ cups chopped walnuts, ⅓ cup canola oil, ⅓ cup honey, and 2 teaspoons pure vanilla extract in a large bowl. Spoon the mixture onto a large jelly roll pan or cookie sheet and bake for 10 minutes. Stir and bake another 5 minutes. Let the granola cool completely, stir in 2 cups raisins or dried cherries, cranberries, and/or blueberries. It'll keep in an airtight container at room temperature for up to 2 weeks.

5. **Rolled oats are not just for the porridge bowl.** If you love a good bowl of oatmeal, seek out simple recipes for oatmeal pancakes, muffins, quick breads, and cookies and see where they lead you.

grits and goat cheese

A warm bowl *of grits with a spoonful of tangy goat cheese is a great way to start the day. Instant polenta or grits (depending on what part of the country you live in—one may be easier to find than the other) cook up in five minutes and are a nice alternative to oatmeal and cream of wheat. Other cheeses may be substituted—sweet Gorgonzola is delicious, as is grated Cheddar.*

4 cups water

½ teaspoon salt, or to taste

1 cup quick-cooking grits or instant polenta

1 tablespoon unsalted butter

Freshly ground black pepper

¼ pound soft, fresh goat cheese

1. Bring the water and salt to a boil in a medium-size saucepan. Slowly stir in the grits or polenta. Reduce the heat to low and cook for 5 minutes, stirring often.

2. Remove pan from the heat, stir in the butter, season with pepper, and taste for salt. Spoon the grits into four bowls and top each with a spoonful of the goat cheese. Serve immediately.

makes 4 servings

pumpkin polenta

Pumpkin and cornmeal *complement each other and are especially nourishing on a frosty fall or winter morning. I like to place a pat of butter on top of each hot portion and let everyone add his or her own maple syrup to taste.*

3½ cups milk

1 cup canned pumpkin puree

1 teaspoon ground ginger

¼ teaspoon salt

1 cup instant grits or polenta

2 tablespoons unsalted butter

Pure maple syrup

1. Combine the milk, pumpkin, ginger, and salt in a medium-size saucepan. Bring to a boil, whisking several times to break up the pumpkin.

2. Slowly stir in the grits or polenta. Reduce the heat to low and cook for 5 minutes, stirring often, until it is thick and smooth. Remove from the heat and spoon the mixture into 4 bowls. Top each with ½ tablespoon of the butter. Serve immediately with maple syrup on the side.

makes 4 servings

honey-date breakfast couscous

Couscous cooked in milk *makes a quick and nutritious breakfast. Other dried fruits and nuts may be substituted if you like. A little bit of heavy cream poured on top of each serving adds richness, but is not necessary.*

2¼ **cups milk**

1 tablespoon unsalted butter

¼ **teaspoon salt**

Pinch of ground nutmeg

One 10-ounce box instant couscous

½ **cup coarsely chopped dates**

¼ **cup coarsely chopped walnuts**

Honey

Heavy cream (optional)

1. Combine the milk, butter, salt, and nutmeg in a medium-size saucepan. Bring to a boil. Stir in the couscous. Remove the pan from the heat and cover. Let stand for 5 minutes, then fluff with a fork. Stir in the dates and walnuts.

2. Divide the couscous among 4 cereal bowls. Serve immediately with honey and heavy cream, if desired, on the side.

makes 4 servings

homemade applesauce

You probably remember *making applesauce with your kindergarten class. What you may have forgotten is how wonderful homemade applesauce can be. If you like yours sweet, use Golden Delicious apples. If you prefer it with a little snap, use Granny Smiths. Serve it alone, or use as a topping for pancakes or French toast.*

8 medium-size apples (about 3 pounds), peeled, cored, and cut into 10 wedges each

½ cup water

½ teaspoon ground cinnamon

3 tablespoons firmly packed brown sugar, or more to taste

1 tablespoon fresh lemon juice

½ teaspoon pure vanilla extract

¼ cup raisins (optional)

1. Combine the apples, water, and cinnamon in a large saucepan and bring to a boil. Cover, reduce the heat to medium-low, and simmer, stirring frequently to prevent sticking, until the apples are very soft, about 15 minutes.

2. Remove the pan from the heat and mash the apples with a fork. Add the brown sugar, lemon juice, vanilla, and raisins, if desired, and stir well to combine. Serve warm or refrigerate up to 2 days and serve cold.

makes 4 to 6 servings

egg and avocado salad with spicy red salsa on the side

6 large eggs

1 medium-size ripe tomato (about ½ pound), cored and cut into ¼-inch dice

½ jalapeño chile, seeded and finely chopped

2 tablespoons fresh lime juice

1 tablespoon finely chopped red onion

1 tablespoon finely chopped fresh cilantro leaves (basil or oregano may be substituted if you like)

½ teaspoon salt, or to taste

1 medium-size ripe avocado

2 tablespoons mayonnaise

Freshly ground black pepper

1. Place the eggs in a small saucepan (they should just fit in one layer). Cover with water and bring to a boil. Cover and remove from the heat. Let the eggs stand in the hot water with the lid on for 18 minutes. Run the eggs under cold water to cool them. Peel, coarsely chop, and place in a medium-size bowl.

2. While the eggs are cooking, prepare the salsa. Combine the tomato, jalapeño, 1 tablespoon of the lime juice, the onion, cilantro, and salt in a small bowl.

3. Peel, pit, and cut the avocado into ¼-inch dice and sprinkle with the remaining tablespoon lime juice. Stir the avocado and mayonnaise into the eggs and season with salt and pepper. Serve the salsa alongside the egg salad, with tortillas or toast if desired.

makes 4 servings

spinach salad with ham and poached eggs

Poached eggs *aren't any more difficult to make than the soft- or hard-cooked varieties, and they make really special breakfast and brunch dishes. You just need to know a few tricks. First, crack each egg that you're going to poach into a small, handled cup. This will make it easy to slide the egg into the boiling water. Second, boil the water in a shallow skillet instead of a saucepan. This will make it easy to retrieve the cooked eggs with a slotted spoon.*

2 teaspoons Dijon mustard

1 tablespoon fresh lemon juice

Salt and freshly ground black pepper

2 tablespoons sour cream or plain low-fat
   yogurt

¼ cup extra-virgin olive oil

1 pound fresh spinach leaves, washed,
   dried, tough stems removed, and leaves
   torn into pieces

2 ounces thinly sliced ham, diced

12 cherry tomatoes, halved

2 tablespoons white vinegar

4 large eggs, each cracked into a small cup

1. Combine the mustard, lemon juice, salt, pepper, sour cream or yogurt, and olive oil in a large salad bowl. Whisk to combine.

2. Toss the spinach, ham, and tomatoes with the dressing. Divide the dressed salad among four salad plates.

continued

3. Fill an 8- or 10-inch skillet nearly to the top with water, add 1 teaspoon of salt and the vinegar, and bring to a boil over high heat.

4. Lower the rim of each cup just into the water, tip the eggs into the water, cover, and remove the skillet from the heat. Poach for exactly 4 minutes. Remove each egg with a slotted spoon and drain well over the pan. Place one on top of each portion of spinach. Serve immediately.

makes 4 servings

a poached egg glossary

Poaching is a relatively austere way to cook an egg since water, and not fat, is the cooking medium. Traditionally, however, people can't seem to resist using poached eggs to create rich and even decadent dishes. Here are descriptions of a few. A recipe for that poached egg essential, hollandaise sauce, follows.

Eggs Benedict. Poached eggs on toasted English muffins, topped with a slice of Canadian bacon and hollandaise.

Eggs Florentine. Poached eggs on toasted English muffins, topped with sautéed spinach and hollandaise.

Eggs Sardou. A New Orleans specialty. Poached eggs on toasted English muffins, topped with artichoke hearts and hollandaise.

Eggs Neptune. Poached eggs on toasted English muffins, topped with chopped shrimp and hollandaise.

Huevos Rancheros. Poached eggs on tortillas, topped with a spicy sauce of tomatoes and chiles and Monterey Jack and run under the broiler for a few seconds to melt the cheese.

classic
hollandaise sauce

4 large egg yolks

**½ cup unsalted butter (1 stick), cut into
  pieces**

1½ tablespoons fresh lemon juice

Salt to taste

1. Fill a small saucepan with 1 inch of water and bring to a bare simmer. Place the yolks in a medium-size stainless steel bowl and place it on top of the simmering water, making sure that the water doesn't touch the bowl. Heat, whisking constantly, until the yolks are slightly thickened, 1 to 2 minutes.

2. Whisk in the butter one piece at a time and continue whisking until the butter is melted and the sauce well blended, 1 to 2 minutes.

3. Whisk in the lemon juice and remove from the heat. Be careful not to overheat the sauce, or it might curdle and become lumpy. Season with salt. Use immediately or reheat by whisking over a saucepan of warm (but not boiling) water.

makes enough for 4 servings of eggs
benedict or one of its variations

dried fruit compote

I like to *soften dried fruit by cooking it in sugar syrup. Star anise and a vanilla bean add exotic notes. If you can't find dried star anise in the spice section of your supermarket, ground cinnamon makes a lovely substitute. Choose your favorites, but stay away from fruit that's been sugared already and berries, which tend to fall apart before the rest of the fruit is ready. Dried fruit compote is nice on its own, on top of waffles or pancakes, or stirred into a favorite hot breakfast cereal.*

1 pound assorted unsweetened dried fruit (apples, apricots, figs, mango, pears, prunes)

2½ cups water

¼ cup sugar

½ vanilla bean, halved lengthwise

1 dried star anise, or ¼ teaspoon cinnamon

1. Combine all ingredients in a medium-size saucepan and bring to a boil. Reduce the heat to medium-low and simmer until the fruit is soft but not falling apart, 10 to 15 minutes.

2. Discard the star anise and vanilla bean. Transfer the fruit and syrup to a medium-size serving bowl and cool to room temperature. Refrigerate until serving time, or up to 3 days.

makes 4 to 6 servings

simple vegetables

Blanched Asparagus with Olive Oil and Manchego Cheese

◆

Blanched Broccoli with Sun-Dried Tomatoes and Lemon Dressing

◆

Broccoli Steamed in Orange Juice

◆

Broccoli Rabe with Garlic-Chile Oil

◆

Boiled Carrots with Butter and Chiles

◆

Blanched Cauliflower with Charmoula

◆

Green Bean Salad with Yogurt and Herbs

◆

Stewed Italian-Style Green Beans

◆

Boiled Kohlrabi with Butter and Bread Crumbs

◆

Blanched Leeks with Ricotta Salata Vinaigrette

◆

Blanched Spinach with Sesame–Rice Wine Vinegar Dressing

◆

continued

Chopped Spiced Zucchini and Olives

◆

Classic French Potato Salad with Tarragon and Chives

◆

New Potatoes with Lemon-Dill Pesto

◆

Sweet Potato Salad with Chili-Lime Dressing

◆

Sour Cream Mashed Potatoes

◆

Acorn Squash and Chipotle Chile Puree

◆

Winter Vegetable Puree

◆

Carrot and Goat Cheese Puree

Boiling is the simplest way to cook vegetables and one of the most versatile. Boiled vegetables can be seasoned in an infinite number of ways. If you want something quick and spare, boil spinach for 2 minutes and toss with a dressing that contains a mere teaspoon of sesame oil. If you want something luscious and indulgent, boil potatoes for 20 minutes and whip with a cup of sour cream. Of course, there are many choices in between.

A dip in boiling water readies vegetables for a variety of mouthwatering treatments. Sometimes, you want your vegetables barely cooked, so that they are crispy and fresh tasting. Blanching, which just means partial cooking in water, works wonderfully for asparagus. The crisp spears become a perfect foil for flavorful olive oil and melting bits of Manchego cheese. Blanching maintains broccoli's freshness, which is enhanced by a sunny dressing of lemon and dried tomatoes. Young green beans cooked this way make a summery salad when dressed with yogurt and herbs.

With harder and/or bitter vegetables like carrots, kohlrabi, cauliflower, and broccoli rabe, raw texture and flavor are not necessarily desirable. You want to cook them long enough so that they become tender, but still retain their shape and color. Check and taste as you cook. Then just drain and toss with something as spicy as charmoula, a Moroccan "pesto" made with mint and cayenne, or as mild as butter and bread crumbs. When boiling potatoes for salad, monitor them often. Potatoes that aren't cooked long enough will be unpleasantly hard and raw tasting; cooked too long, they become mushy and will disintegrate.

In the case of mashed potatoes and root-vegetable purees, the vegetables must be cooked so that they are soft enough to be mashed or processed until completely smooth.

continued

It is amazing to me how boiled potatoes, squash, turnips, and celery root are transformed from soggy, starchy lumps into deeply satisfying side dishes that are often preferred to the main course. Potatoes whipped in a mixer with sour cream are smooth and slightly piquant. Squash whirled in a food processor with chipotle chiles makes an eye-opening puree. Unglamorous winter vegetables—parsnips, leeks, celery root—become surprisingly interesting when blended together.

blanched asparagus with olive oil and manchego cheese

Manchego *is a wonderful Spanish cheese with a flavor and texture akin to Parmesan or dried Jack, but a little mellower. Crumbled bits of Manchego melting on the warm asparagus spears make a perfect side dish for Squid with Saffron Couscous (page 213) or Chicken and Rice (page 191).*

1½ pounds asparagus, tough ends trimmed

1 teaspoon salt, plus more to taste

2 tablespoons extra-virgin olive oil, or more to taste

¼ cup crumbled Manchego or freshly grated Parmesan cheese

1 tablespoon finely chopped fresh parsley leaves

Freshly ground black pepper to taste

1. Bring a large pot of water to a boil. Add the asparagus and salt and boil until just tender, 2 to 4 minutes, depending on thickness.

2. Drain the asparagus and return to the hot pot. Toss with the olive oil, cheese, and parsley and season with salt and pepper. Serve immediately.

makes 4 servings

blanched broccoli with sun-dried tomatoes and lemon dressing

Grated zest *imparts a tart citrus flavor here. Sun-dried tomatoes add color and sweetness.*

1 teaspoon salt, plus more to taste

1 head broccoli (about 1 pound), stems discarded, flower separated into small florets

2 tablespoons extra-virgin olive oil, or more to taste

10 sun-dried tomatoes packed in oil, drained and finely chopped

2 teaspoons grated lemon zest

1 garlic clove, peeled and finely chopped

Freshly ground black pepper to taste

1. Bring a medium-size saucepan of water to a boil. Add the 1 teaspoon salt and broccoli, and boil until the broccoli is just tender, 3 to 4 minutes.

2. Drain and place in a medium-size serving bowl. Stir in the olive oil, tomatoes, lemon zest, and garlic and season with salt and pepper. Serve warm or refrigerate and serve cold or at room temperature.

makes 4 servings

broccoli steamed in orange juice

This ingenious recipe *is adapted from Colin Spencer's beautiful and informative* The Vegetable Book. *The broccoli is cooked above, rather than in, the boiling liquid so that it doesn't turn brown from contact with the acid in the juice.*

1 cup orange juice

1 cup water

1 teaspoon grated orange zest

½ teaspoon Tabasco sauce

½ teaspoon salt, plus more to taste

½ teaspoon sugar

1 head broccoli (about 1 pound), stems discarded, flower separated into small florets

1 tablespoon unsalted butter (optional)

1. Combine the orange juice, water, orange zest, Tabasco, salt, and sugar in a medium-size saucepan. Place a vegetable steamer above the liquid and place the broccoli florets in the steamer. Bring to a boil, cover, and steam until tender, about 5 minutes. Lift the steamer from the pot, place the broccoli in a medium-size serving bowl, and cover with aluminum foil to keep warm.

2. Boil the liquid, uncovered, until it is reduced and thickened, about 3 minutes. Remove from the heat, stir in the butter if desired, and season with salt. Pour the sauce over the broccoli and serve immediately.

makes 4 servings

broccoli rabe with garlic-chile oil

The bitter flavor *of boiled broccoli rabe is enhanced by the equally strong flavors of garlic and chiles. I like the subtle taste of crushed garlic cloves steeped in oil for several hours, but if you like a stronger flavor or are in a rush, just stir the oil, pepper flakes, and 1 finely chopped garlic clove into the cooked broccoli rabe instead of infusing the oil.*

6 garlic cloves, peeled and crushed with the back of a chef's knife

½ teaspoon hot red pepper flakes

¼ cup extra-virgin olive oil

1 head broccoli rabe (about 1 pound), washed and tough stems removed

1 teaspoon salt, plus more to taste

1. Place the garlic and red pepper flakes in a small bowl and cover with the olive oil. Let stand at room temperature for at least 6 hours or up to 1 day.

2. Bring a large saucepan of water to a boil. Add the broccoli rabe and salt and boil until tender and wilted, about 2 minutes. Drain well in a colander, pat dry with paper towels, and place in a serving bowl. Remove the garlic cloves from the oil and discard. Pour the seasoned oil over the broccoli rabe and toss to coat. Season with salt. Serve immediately.

makes 4 servings

boiled carrots with butter and chiles

The sweetness *of carrots is heightened by butter and hot chiles. Using baby carrots eliminates peeling and chopping.*

I pound peeled baby carrots

I teaspoon salt, plus more to taste

2 tablespoons unsalted butter

I jalapeño chile, seeded and finely chopped

2 teaspoons fresh lime juice

I teaspoon grated lime zest

½ teaspoon ground cumin

I. Bring a large pot of water to a boil. Add the carrots and salt and boil until tender but not mushy, about 10 minutes.

2. Drain the carrots and place in a serving bowl. Add the butter, jalapeño, lime juice and zest, and cumin and season with salt. Gently toss to combine. Serve immediately.

makes 4 servings

blanched cauliflower with charmoula

Charmoula *is a Moroccan sauce of herbs, spices, and olive oil, traditionally used as a marinade. Here I toss it with blanched cauliflower. This makes a lively accompaniment for plain grilled chicken or fish.*

I medium-size cauliflower, tough stems removed and cut into small florets

I teaspoon salt, plus more to taste

I cup tightly packed fresh cilantro leaves

½ cup tightly packed fresh mint leaves

I garlic clove, peeled

¼ cup extra-virgin olive oil

2 tablespoons fresh lemon juice

I teaspoon sweet paprika

½ teaspoon ground cumin

¼ teaspoon cayenne pepper

I. Bring a large saucepan of water to a boil. Add the cauliflower and salt and cook until tender, 5 to 7 minutes. Drain and place in a large bowl.

2. Combine the cilantro, mint, and garlic in the work bowl of a food processor or blender and process until finely chopped, scraping down the sides of the bowl once or twice as necessary. With the motor running, add the olive oil and lemon juice. Scrape the mixture into a small bowl and stir in the paprika, cumin, cayenne, and salt to

taste. Stir the charmoula into the warm cauliflower until well coated with the mixture. Serve warm or refrigerate for up to I day and serve cold or at room temperature.

makes 4 servings

green bean salad with yogurt and herbs

Yogurt *is a tart background for sweet, young green beans. A little sour cream lends richness without a lot of fat. Re-whisk the dressing before mixing with green beans to avoid separation.*

1 pound green beans, ends trimmed

1 teaspoon salt, plus more to taste

½ cup plain low-fat yogurt

2 tablespoons sour cream

2 tablespoons finely chopped fresh parsley leaves

2 tablespoons finely chopped fresh basil leaves

Freshly ground black pepper

1. Bring a large saucepan of water to a boil. Add the beans and salt and cook until tender but not mushy, 2 to 3 minutes. Drain and cool to room temperature.

2. Whisk together the yogurt, sour cream, parsley, and basil in a small bowl. Toss the cooled beans with the dressing, season with salt and pepper, and serve immediately.

makes 4 servings

stewed italian-style green beans

When I get slender, *just-picked green beans from the farm, I simply blanch them and toss with dressing. Older, tougher beans respond well to longer cooking, which softens and flavors them. This recipe is adapted from my husband's wonderful book* The Complete Italian Vegetarian Cookbook, *so you can be sure that it's delicious.*

I cup canned crushed tomatoes

I pound green beans, ends trimmed

2 tablespoons extra-virgin olive oil

I medium-size onion, peeled and finely chopped

3 garlic cloves, peeled and finely chopped

I tablespoon red wine vinegar

2 tablespoons chopped fresh tarragon leaves

Salt and freshly ground black pepper to taste

I. Place the tomatoes, beans, olive oil, onion, garlic, and vinegar in a large skil-let. Stir well to combine. Bring to a boil, cover, and reduce the heat to medium-low. Simmer until the beans are tender but not mushy, 25 to 30 minutes.

2. Stir in the tarragon, season with salt and pepper, and serve.

makes 4 servings

boiled kohlrabi with butter and bread crumbs

I love the sweet, *nutty flavor of boiled kohlrabi (it tastes like very mild cauliflower) tossed with a little butter and some bread crumbs for textural contrast. Store-bought croutons make great bread crumbs. I buy mine at a local deli where they make them from homemade bread. Since croutons are already crunchy, there's no need to toast them before using—just grind for a few seconds in a food processor.*

½ **cup unseasoned croutons**

4 small kohlrabi bulbs

I teaspoon salt, plus more to taste

2 tablespoons unsalted butter

I tablespoon finely chopped fresh parsley leaves

Freshly ground black pepper to taste

I. Place the croutons in the work bowl of a food processor and pulse several times until finely ground. Set aside.

2. Trim the stems from the kohlrabi and peel the tough skin from the bulbs with a vegetable peeler. Cut into ¼-inch-thick matchsticks.

3. Bring a large saucepan of water to a boil. Add the kohlrabi and the salt and cook until tender, 8 to 10 minutes.

4. Drain and place in a serving bowl. Toss with the bread crumbs, butter, and parsley, season with salt and pepper, and serve immediately.

makes 4 servings

blanched leeks with
ricotta salata vinaigrette

Thin strands *of leek become mellow when boiled for just a few minutes. A vinaigrette and a sprinkling of basil and cheese turn them into a simple but interesting side dish. Ricotta salata is available in most supermarkets and Italian groceries. Feta cheese may be substituted, if you like.*

2 tablespoons extra-virgin olive oil

1 tablespoon red wine vinegar

1 teaspoon Dijon mustard

1¼ teaspoons salt

Freshly ground black pepper

6 leeks

2 ounces ricotta salata, crumbled

2 tablespoons chopped fresh basil leaves

1. Combine the olive oil, vinegar, mustard, ¼ teaspoon of the salt, and pepper to taste in a small bowl. Set aside.

2. Cut off the roots and the tough dark green portion of the leeks. Discard the tough outer layers. Rinse away any dirt under cold water. Slice each leek lengthwise into quarters.

3. Bring a large saucepan of water to a boil. Add the leeks and the remaining teaspoon salt and cook until just tender, 2 to 3 minutes. Drain and pat dry with paper towels.

4. Combine the leeks, dressing, ricotta salata, and basil in a large serving bowl. Serve at room temperature or refrigerate and serve cold.

makes 4 servings

blanched spinach with sesame–rice wine vinegar dressing

Mild blanched spinach, *simply dressed, pairs well with assertively flavored main courses like Beef Short Ribs with Exotic Spices (page 170).*

1 teaspoon Asian sesame oil

1 teaspoon soy sauce

1 teaspoon rice wine vinegar

½ teaspoon peeled and finely chopped fresh gingerroot

¼ teaspoon hot red pepper flakes

4 cups water

2 pounds fresh spinach, washed and tough stems removed

1. Combine the sesame oil, soy sauce, vinegar, ginger, and red pepper flakes in a small bowl.

2. Bring the water to a boil in a large pot. Add the spinach, cover, and cook until it begins to wilt, about 2 minutes. Dump the spinach into a colander and gently press it with the back of a large spoon to drain excess water.

3. Place the spinach in a medium-size serving bowl and toss well with the dressing. Serve warm or refrigerate and serve chilled.

makes 4 servings

chopped spiced zucchini and olives

This boiled *vegetable dish is anything but bland.*

1 teaspoon salt

1½ pounds zucchini, ends trimmed and cut into ½-inch-thick rounds

2 tablespoons fresh lemon juice

2 tablespoons extra-virgin olive oil

2 garlic cloves, peeled and finely chopped

¼ teaspoon ground coriander

¼ teaspoon fennel seeds

8 Kalamata or other large black olives, pitted and coarsely chopped

Freshly ground black pepper to taste

1. Bring a medium-size saucepan of water to a boil. Add the salt and zucchini, and boil until the zucchini is softened, about 5 minutes.

2. Drain the zucchini in a colander and press with the back of a large spoon to remove any excess water.

3. Place the zucchini in the work bowl of a food processor and pulse once or twice to coarsely chop. Alternatively, coarsely chop by hand with a large chef's knife. Do not overprocess or -chop; the zucchini should be a little bit chunky.

4. Scrape the zucchini into a medium-size serving bowl, stir in the rest of the ingredients, and serve warm or refrigerate for up to 5 hours and bring to room temperature before serving.

makes 4 servings

classic french potato salad with tarragon and chives

I like a splash *of tarragon vinegar here to emphasize the fresh tarragon, but if you don't have any on hand, just white wine vinegar is fine.*

2 pounds medium-size red potatoes

2 teaspoons salt, plus more to taste

2 tablespoons white wine vinegar

I teaspoon tarragon vinegar

6 tablespoons extra-virgin olive oil

I tablespoon Dijon mustard

I small shallot, peeled and finely chopped

2 tablespoons finely chopped fresh chives

I tablespoon finely chopped fresh tarragon leaves

Freshly ground black pepper

I. Place the potatoes in a large pot, cover generously with water, add the salt, and bring to a boil. Continue to boil until just tender when pierced with a sharp paring knife, 25 to 30 minutes. Drain and cool slightly. Slice the potatoes into ¼-inch-thick rounds, leaving the skin on. Place the slices in a large bowl and sprinkle with the vinegars.

2. Whisk together the olive oil, mustard, shallot, chives, and tarragon in a small bowl. Gently stir the dressing into the potatoes, then season with salt and pepper. Serve warm or refrigerate up to 24 hours and bring to room temperature before serving.

makes 4 servings

new potatoes with lemon-dill pesto

Basil pesto *is very good as a dressing for boiled potatoes, but a pesto made with dill and lemon is just perfect. Serve this salad as a harbinger of spring with Perfect Poached Salmon (page 11).*

½ cup tightly packed fresh dill leaves

½ cup tightly packed fresh parsley leaves

1 small garlic clove, peeled and coarsely chopped

2 teaspoons grated lemon zest

⅓ cup extra-virgin olive oil

Salt and freshly ground black pepper to taste

2 pounds red new potatoes

1. Combine the dill, parsley, garlic, and lemon zest in the work bowl of a food processor or blender and process until finely chopped, scraping down the sides of the bowl once or twice as necessary. With the motor running, add the olive oil in a slow stream. Scrape the pesto into a small bowl, season with salt and pepper, and set aside.

2. Place the potatoes in a large pot, cover generously with water, add 2 teaspoons salt, and bring to a boil. Cook until just tender when pierced with a sharp paring knife, 10 to 20 minutes, depending on the size and age of the potatoes.

3. Drain the potatoes in a colander. Cut into halves or quarters, depending on size, and transfer to a large serving bowl. Toss with the pesto and serve warm, or refrigerate and bring to room temperature before serving.

makes 4 servings

sweet potato salad with chili-lime dressing

This is a great *summer salad, perfect with all kinds of barbecue and grilled foods. It's also a wonderful way to brighten up a winter dinner of broiled chicken or beef.*

2 pounds sweet potatoes, peeled and
    cut into 1-inch chunks

⅓ cup extra-virgin olive oil

2 tablespoons fresh lime juice

1 teaspoon chili powder

½ teaspoon ground cumin

¼ cup finely chopped fresh cilantro leaves

Salt and freshly ground black pepper to taste

½ medium-size red bell pepper,
    seeded and cut into ¼-inch dice

4 scallions, white and light green parts,
    finely chopped

1. Place the sweet potatoes in a large saucepan and cover with water. Bring to a boil and cook until just tender, 7 to 10 minutes (don't overcook or your salad will be mushy and falling apart). Drain and transfer to a large bowl.

2. While the potatoes are cooking, make the dressing. Whisk together the olive oil, lime juice, chili powder, cumin, cilantro, salt, and pepper in a small bowl. Add the red bell pepper and scallions to the potatoes and toss with the dressing. Season again with salt and pepper. Serve warm or refrigerate and bring to room temperature before serving.

makes 6 servings

sour cream mashed potatoes

I make my *mashed potatoes the way my mom taught me, using sour cream instead of butter and mashing and mixing them with the paddle attachment in an electric mixer. Sour cream gives the potatoes piquancy as well as richness. The mixer whips them up so that they're fluffy beyond belief. You can reheat the potatoes in a microwave or in a double boiler if they cool off while you're making them or you'd like to make them several hours ahead of serving time.*

2 pounds Idaho or Yukon Gold potatoes, peeled and cut into 2-inch pieces

½ teaspoon salt, plus more to taste

I cup sour cream

Freshly ground black pepper to taste

I. Place the potatoes and salt in a large saucepan and cover with cold water. Bring to a boil and cook over medium-high heat until the potatoes are soft when pierced through with a knife, 15 to 20 minutes.

2. Drain the potatoes well (too much water will make them gummy instead of fluffy) and place them in the bowl of an electric mixer fitted with the paddle attachment or mash by hand with a potato masher. Add the sour cream and mix on low or whisk by hand until smooth. Season with salt and pepper and serve immediately.

makes 6 servings

flavoring mashed potatoes

There are as many ways to dress up mashed potatoes as there are Baskin-Robbins ice cream flavors, some of them obvious (garlic), some a little bit out there (lox). Here are a few of my favorites.

Garlic Mashed Potatoes: Add 3 peeled garlic cloves to the pan along with the potatoes and mash with the potatoes. Proceed with the recipe for Sour Cream Mashed potatoes.

Sour Cream Mashed Potatoes and Leeks with Horseradish: Decrease the potatoes to 1½ pounds and add ½ pound leeks, white part only, well washed, to the pot. Proceed with the recipe for Sour Cream Mashed Potatoes, adding 1 to 2 tablespoons prepared horseradish, to your taste, to the potatoes and leeks when they go into the mixer.

Chili Mashed Potatoes: Add 2 teaspoons chili powder, or more to taste, to the potatoes when they go into the mixer. Proceed with the recipe for Sour Cream Mashed Potatoes.

Gorgonzola Mashed Potatoes: Stir in ½ cup crumbled Gorgonzola after you mix the potatoes with the sour cream.

Parmesan and Basil Mashed Potatoes: Stir in ¾ cup freshly grated Parmesan and 2 tablespoons finely chopped fresh basil leaves after you mix the potatoes with the sour cream.

Dill and Chive Mashed Potatoes: Stir in 2 tablespoons chopped fresh dill and ¼ cup chopped fresh chives after you mix the potatoes with the sour cream.

Prosciutto and Parsley Mashed Potatoes: Stir in 1 cup finely chopped prosciutto and 2 tablespoons finely chopped fresh parsley leaves after you mix the potatoes with the sour cream.

acorn squash and chipotle chile puree

This spicy puree *lends a Southwestern flavor to plain grilled meat or roast chicken. Chipotle chiles vary in heat, so add the chile a little at a time until you reach the desired level.*

Here's the simplest way to separate the squash from its skin: Cut the squash crosswise in half. Scrape out the seeds and discard. Place each half cut side down on a cutting board. With a sharp chef's knife or serrated knife, remove the skin in strips, cutting from top to bottom and working all the way around each squash half. Cut the flesh into ½-inch cubes.

1 medium-size acorn squash (about 2 pounds), peeled and cut into 1-inch cubes

¼ canned chipotle chile in adobo, or more to taste

¼ cup sour cream (optional)

Salt and freshly ground black pepper to taste

1. Place the squash in a large saucepan and cover with water. Bring to a boil, reduce the heat to medium-low, and simmer, uncovered, until soft, about 10 minutes.

2. Drain squash well and place in the work bowl of a food processor, with the

chile and sour cream, if desired. Process until smooth, scraping down the sides of the bowl once or twice as necessary. If the puree is not hot enough, add another ¼ of a chile and process. Season with salt and pepper and serve immediately.

makes 4 servings

winter vegetable puree

The addition of *celery root, parsnips, and leeks to boiled potatoes gives this puree a little dimension. Serve as you would plain mashed potatoes alongside roast chicken or Hearty Beef Stew (page 165).*

1 medium-size celery root, trimmed, peeled, and cut into ½-inch cubes

1 medium-size parsnip, peeled and cut into 1-inch cubes

4 leeks, white parts only, washed and cut into 1-inch pieces

2 medium-size baking potatoes, peeled and cut into 1-inch cubes

2 to 4 tablespoons unsalted butter, to your taste

Salt and freshly ground black pepper to taste

1. Combine the celery root, parsnip, leeks, and potatoes in a large saucepan and cover with water. Bring to a boil, reduce the heat to medium-low, and simmer, uncovered, until soft, 12 to 15 minutes.

2. Drain vegetables well and place in the work bowl of a food processor, along with the butter. Process until smooth, scraping down the sides of the bowl once or twice as necessary. Season with salt and pepper and serve immediately.

makes 4 servings

carrot and goat cheese puree

Sour cream or *crème fraîche may be substituted for the goat cheese here. Be generous with the pepper—a little heat contrasts well with the sweet and tangy carrot mixture.*

1 pound carrots, peeled, trimmed, and cut into 1-inch pieces

3 ounces goat cheese, crumbled

2 scallions, white and light green parts, finely chopped

Salt and ground black pepper to taste

1. Place the carrots in a large saucepan and cover with water. Bring to a boil, reduce the heat, and simmer, uncovered, until soft, 10 to 12 minutes. Drain well and place in a food processor, along with the goat cheese. Process until smooth, scraping down the side of the bowl once or twice as necessary.

2. Stir in the scallions, season with salt and pepper, and serve immediately.

makes 4 servings

simple soups

Curried Cream of Carrot Soup

◆

Butternut Squash Soup

◆

African Peanut Soup

◆

Italian Tomato and Bread Soup

◆

Manhattan Clam Chowder

◆

Saffron Mussel Bisque

◆

Chicken and Herbed Dumpling Soup

◆

Stracciatella

◆

Avgolemono

◆

Sausage, Barley, and Spinach Soup

This chapter is devoted to that quintessential boiled food, soup. Here is the heart and soul of *Just Add Water*. A few humble ingredients, a big pot, a low flame, and you've got a homemade, nourishing dinner. Here are my favorite simple soups, including a delectably spicy Curried Cream of Carrot Soup made with coconut milk; a peasant-style Italian Tomato and Bread Soup that could claim a place on the menu at any fashionable trattoria; and an all-American Chicken and Herbed Dumpling Soup—all of them just boil and serve.

The first four recipes are for pureed vegetable soups. Pureeing simmered ingredients somehow lends soup a more complex flavor than it has a right to have. Butternut Squash Soup is as easy to make as a bowl of instant noodles, but refined enough to serve at Thanksgiving dinner. Just simmer chunks of squash and leeks in chicken broth and water, then puree. Stir in a little cream for some richness if you like.

Pureeing hot soup in a blender can be messy and even dangerous if you overfill the blender pitcher. The agitation of the motor can send a geyser of boiling liquid shooting out of the spout. Never fill the blender more than halfway with hot soup. Puree in batches, pouring each finished batch into a bowl and then combining them in the soup pot when you're through to avoid bandaged hands and soup on the ceiling. You can also use a hand-held immersion blender, and puree the soup right in the pot. But again, make sure your pot isn't filled so high that it will overflow when you turn the blender on.

Next to pureed soups in simplicity are shellfish-based soups. Clams and mussels quickly create a flavorful stock when steamed in just a little wine or water. Rustic Manhattan

Clam Chowder has a tomato base and chunks of potato for bulk and flavor. Saffron Mussel Bisque is rich and luxurious.

No matter how thoroughly you wash them before cooking, shellfish always leave a little sand in the cooking liquid. It is essential to strain the broth after the clams or mussels are removed. Line a colander with several layers of cheesecloth or paper towels and pour the broth through the colander and into a saucepan.

Canned chicken broth is fine in any of the vegetable soups. It has enough flavor to give these soups a little dimension, and certainly is a convenience if you don't have homemade stock on hand. I always buy low-sodium broth so I can control the saltiness of the finished dish. Chicken soup, however, requires home-made stock, since what's being showcased is the chicken flavor of the stock itself. Making good, strong chicken stock is just a matter of bringing chicken and water to boil. Once you know how to do this, you can create an amazing variety of chicken soups just by adding ingredients to the simmering broth. The making of the stock is included in the recipes for chicken soups in this chapter. If you want to try some chicken soup variations of your own, begin with homemade chicken stock (page 8) rather than canned broth.

curried cream of carrot soup

Unsweetened coconut milk, *rather than heavy cream, lends this quick soup a tropical sweetness. I like my soup pretty spicy, but if you don't, cut the curry powder in half.*

2 pounds carrots, peeled, trimmed, and cut into 1-inch pieces

1 medium-size onion, peeled and finely chopped

2 tablespoons curry powder

1 teaspoon ground ginger

2 cups homemade chicken stock (page 8) or canned low-sodium chicken broth

4 cups water

1 cup unsweetened coconut milk

2 tablespoons finely chopped fresh cilantro leaves

Salt and freshly ground black pepper to taste

1. Combine the carrots, onion, curry powder, ginger, chicken stock, and water in a large pot. Bring to a boil, reduce the heat to medium-low, and simmer until the carrots are very soft, 20 to 25 minutes.

2. Puree the soup, in batches if necessary, in a blender. Return to the pot and stir in the coconut milk and cilantro. Heat through, season with salt and pepper, and serve.

makes 6 to 8 servings

butternut squash soup

Rather than halve *the squash and scoop out the flesh, I find this method easier: With a sharp serrated knife, cut through the squash to separate the elongated top portion from the bulbous bottom portion. Cut away the skin from both portions, working from top to bottom, in thin strips. Cut each portion in half. Scoop out the seeds from the bottom portion. Cut the squash into 1-inch cubes. Acorn squash or pumpkin may be substituted for butternut squash, if you like.*

1 medium-size butternut squash (about 2 pounds), peeled, seeded, and cut into 1-inch cubes

1 leek, white part only, washed and coarsely chopped

4 fresh sage leaves, finely chopped

2 cups homemade chicken stock (page 8) or canned low-sodium chicken broth

3 cups water

Salt and freshly ground black pepper

½ cup heavy cream (optional)

1. Combine the squash, leek, sage, chicken stock, water, salt, and pepper in a large pot, bring to a boil, cover, reduce the heat to medium-low, and simmer until the squash is very soft, about 30 minutes.

2. Puree the soup, in batches if necessary, in a blender. Return to the pot, add the heavy cream if desired, season with salt and pepper, heat through, and serve.

makes 4 to 6 servings

african peanut soup

A spicy soup *enriched with ground peanuts. Serve with fluffy biscuits and a salad for a complete meal.*

1 medium-size onion, finely chopped

2 medium-size sweet potatoes, peeled and cut into ¼-inch dice

¼ teaspoon cayenne pepper, or to taste

6 cups homemade chicken stock (page 8) or canned low-sodium chicken broth

2 cups water

1½ cups dry-roasted peanuts

Salt and freshly ground black pepper to taste

2 tablespoons chopped fresh cilantro leaves

1. Combine the onion, sweet potatoes, cayenne, chicken stock, and water in a large pot, bring to a boil, cover, reduce the heat to medium-low, and simmer until the vegetables are soft, about 30 minutes.

2. Puree the soup and peanuts in a blender, in batches if necessary. If the soup is too thick, add some water until it reaches the desired consistency. Return to the pot and season with salt and black pepper. Heat through and stir in the cilantro just before serving.

makes 4 to 6 servings

italian tomato and bread soup

Italians use *day-old bread to soak up this garlicky tomato soup. I like this soup hot in the winter, when I use canned tomatoes, or at room temperature in the summer, when I use ripe ones from my local farmstand.*

3 garlic cloves

4 slices stale country bread

1½ pounds ripe plum tomatoes, peeled, seeded, and coarsely chopped; or one 28-ounce can whole tomatoes, drained and coarsely chopped

2 tablespoons extra-virgin olive oil, plus extra for drizzling

¼ cup finely chopped fresh parsley leaves

2 cups homemade chicken stock (page 8) or canned low-sodium chicken broth

2 tablespoons finely chopped fresh basil leaves

Salt and freshly ground black pepper to taste

Freshly grated Parmesan cheese (optional)

1. Peel the garlic cloves. Rub the bread on both sides with one of the cloves. Tear the bread into bite-size pieces. Finely chop the remaining 2 cloves.

2. Combine the chopped garlic, tomatoes, olive oil, and parsley in a medium-size saucepan. Bring to a boil, reduce the heat to medium-low, and simmer until the tomatoes are thickened, about 5 minutes. Add the chicken stock, return to a boil, and boil for 2 minutes. Stir in the basil and season with salt and pepper.

3. Divide the bread among four soup bowls. Pour the soup over the bread. Serve hot or at room temperature with olive oil for drizzling and grated Parmesan cheese, if desired.

makes 4 servings

manhattan clam chowder

Manhattan Clam Chowder, *with its tomato base, is flavorful and light. If you prefer your chowder New England style, omit the tomatoes, stir in 1 cup heavy cream with the clams, heat through, and serve.*

2 pounds littleneck clams

1 cup canned crushed tomatoes

1½ cups water

4 garlic cloves, peeled and crushed

1 medium-size onion, peeled and finely chopped

2 large potatoes, peeled and cut into ¼-inch dice

2 tablespoons finely chopped fresh parsley leaves

Salt and freshly ground black pepper to taste

1. Rinse the clams by placing them in a large bowl, filling it with cold water, and draining. Do this several times until the water looks clear. Discard any clams that will not close or that have broken shells.

2. Combine the clams, tomatoes, water, and garlic in a large pot. Cover, turn the heat to high, and cook, stirring once or twice, until the clams have all opened up, 5 to 7 minutes. Remove the clams with a slotted spoon and place in a large bowl. Discard any clams that do not open. Working over the bowl, remove the meat from the shells and discard the shells. Coarsely chop the clams and set aside.

3. Add any liquid from the clam bowl to the cooking liquid. Pour the liquid

through a colander lined with cheesecloth or paper towels and into a large
measuring cup, pressing down on the
solids with the back of the spoon to
extract all the liquid. Add enough water
to make 4 cups liquid. Pour the liquid
into a saucepan, add the onion and pota-

toes, and bring to a boil. Cover and simmer until the potatoes are tender, 8 to
10 minutes. Stir in the clams and parsley,
season with salt and pepper,
and serve.

makes 4 servings

saffron mussel bisque

Although inexpensive, *mussels make a luxurious seafood bisque enriched with egg yolks and seasoned with saffron. To prevent curdling, whisk a little of the hot broth into the egg yolk mixture before you stir the yolks into the soup.*

2 pounds mussels

1½ cups dry white wine

3 garlic cloves, peeled and crushed

1 cup half-and-half

2 large egg yolks

½ teaspoon saffron threads

1 tablespoon finely chopped fresh chives

Salt and freshly ground black pepper to taste

1. Rinse the mussels by placing them in a large bowl, filling it with cold water, and draining. Do this several times until the water looks clear. Discard any mussels that will not close or have broken shells.

2. Combine the mussels, wine, and garlic in a large pot. Cover, turn the heat to high, and cook, stirring once or twice, until the mussels have all opened up, 7 to 10 minutes. Remove the mussels with a slotted spoon and place in a large bowl. Discard any mussels that will not open. Working over the bowl, remove the meat from the shells and discard the shells. Coarsely chop the mussels and set aside.

3. Add any liquid from the mussel bowl to the cooking liquid. Pour the liquid through a colander lined with cheesecloth or paper towels and into a large measuring cup. Add water to make 3 cups liquid.

continued

Pour the liquid into a medium-size saucepan and bring to a bare simmer.

4. Whisk together the half-and-half and egg yolks in a medium-size bowl. Gradually whisk about a cup of the simmering cooking liquid into the mixture, then whisk the egg mixture back into the pot. Stir in the saffron and continue to whisk until the soup thickens slightly, 2 to 3 minutes. Stir in the mussels and chives, season with salt and pepper, and serve.

makes 4 servings

chicken and herbed dumpling soup

This is basically *just nice, strong chicken stock with fluffy, fresh-tasting dumplings floating in it. Make the soup ahead of time, refrigerate, and skim off the fat. Cook the dumplings in the reheated soup just before serving.*

4 pounds chicken backs, wings, and/or whole legs

3½ quarts water

1 medium-size onion, peeled and cut into medium-size dice

1 large bunch fresh dill

2 bay leaves

2 teaspoons salt

4 medium-size carrots, peeled and cut into 2-inch lengths

4 small turnips, peeled and cut into ¼-inch-thick slices

Freshly ground black pepper to taste

FOR THE DUMPLINGS

2 cups all-purpose flour

1 tablespoon baking powder

¾ teaspoon salt

2 tablespoons chopped fresh tarragon leaves

2 tablespoons chopped fresh parsley leaves

3 tablespoons unsalted butter

1 cup milk

1. Place the chicken and water in a large pot. Bring to a boil, reduce the heat to medium-low, and simmer for 7 minutes, using a mesh skimmer to remove any

foam that rises to the surface. Add the onion, dill, bay leaves, and salt and simmer for another 3 hours.

2. Strain the broth; discard the bones. Skim off the fat.

3. Bring the broth back to a boil and add the carrots and turnips. Reduce the heat to medium-low, cover, and simmer for about 5 minutes. Season with salt and pepper.

4. Make the dumplings. Mix the flour, baking powder, salt, tarragon, and parsley in a medium-size bowl. Heat the butter and milk together in a small saucepan to a bare simmer and add to the dry ingredients. Mix with a fork just until the mixture comes together.

5. Bring the soup to a simmer and drop in rounded tablespoonfuls of the dumpling mixture. Cover and cook until the dumplings are tender and risen, about 10 minutes. Serve immediately.

makes 6 to 8 servings

stracciatella

Stracciatella *is Italian comfort food—chicken soup with tender bits of scrambled eggs and cheese.*

4 pounds chicken backs, wings, and/or whole legs

3½ quarts water

1 medium-size onion, peeled and cut into medium-size dice

1 large bunch fresh dill

2 bay leaves

1 teaspoon salt, plus more to taste

Freshly ground black pepper to taste

4 large eggs

¼ cup freshly grated Parmesan cheese

¼ cup finely chopped fresh parsley leaves

Pinch of ground nutmeg

1. Place the chicken and water in a large pot. Bring to a boil, reduce the heat to medium-low, and simmer for 10 minutes, using a mesh skimmer to remove any foam that rises to the surface. Add the onion, dill, bay leaves, and salt and simmer, partially covered, for 3 hours.

2. Strain the broth; discard the bones. Skim off the fat. Season with salt and pepper. Bring the broth back to a boil.

3. Whisk together the eggs, cheese, parsley, nutmeg, and salt and pepper to taste in a medium-size bowl.

4. Pour the eggs into the boiling stock. Let the eggs stand in the broth without mixing until they are set, about 30 seconds, then break them up with a fork. Season with salt and pepper and serve immediately.

makes 6 to 8 servings

avgolemono

This soup is a classic *of Greek country cooking. Although bulked up with rice, avgolemono still tastes fresh and light because of abundant lemon juice and parsley.*

4 pounds chicken backs, wings, and/or
   whole legs

3½ quarts water

1 medium-size onion, peeled and cut into
   medium-size dice

1 large bunch fresh dill

2 bay leaves

1 teaspoon salt, plus more to taste

1 cup long-grain white rice

4 large eggs

1 cup fresh lemon juice

⅓ cup chopped fresh parsley leaves

Freshly ground white pepper to taste

1. Place the chicken and water in a large pot. Bring to a boil, reduce the heat to medium-low, and simmer for 7 minutes, using a mesh skimmer to remove any foam that rises to the surface. Add the onion, dill, bay leaves, and salt and simmer, partially covered, for 3 hours.

2. Strain the broth; discard the bones. Skim off the fat. Bring the broth back to a boil. Add the rice and return to a simmer; reduce the heat to medium-low and cook partially covered until the rice is tender, about 20 minutes.

3. Whisk together the eggs, lemon juice, and parsley. Whisk the egg mixture into the kettle and continue whisking to break up clumps of rice and incorporate the eggs. Heat the soup through, but do not allow it to come to a boil. Season with salt and pepper and serve immediately.

makes 6 to 8 servings

chicken soup

Chicken Stock (page 8) can quickly become chicken soup with the addition of a few ingredients:

Chicken Noodle: Poach 1 whole boneless, skinless chicken breast (page 10); cool and shred. In 2 tablespoons olive oil over medium heat, cook, stirring, 1 chopped carrot, 1 chopped onion, and 1 chopped celery stalk until soft. Bring 1 recipe chicken stock to a simmer. Add the vegetables, chicken, and 3 cups cooked egg noodles. Season with salt and pepper, heat through, and serve.

Chicken Vegetable: Add 4 cups of any combination of asparagus, peas, zucchini, seeded and chopped tomatoes, and/or lima beans to Chicken Noodle Soup. Simmer until tender. Stir in 2 tablespoons chopped fresh basil or parsley leaves and serve.

Matzoh Ball: Cook 20 baby carrots in 1 recipe simmering Chicken Stock until tender, 10 to 15 minutes. Combine 4 large eggs, ½ cup water, ¼ cup vegetable oil, 1 cup matzoh meal, salt, and pepper in a large bowl. Refrigerate until solid, about 1 hour. With moistened hands, form into walnut-size balls and drop into the simmering broth. Cover and cook through, about 15 minutes.

Egg Drop Soup: Thicken 1 recipe Chicken Stock by stirring 2 tablespoons cornstarch mixed with 2 tablespoons water into the simmering broth. Season with 1 tablespoon soy sauce. Beat 4 large eggs and slowly pour the eggs into the simmering broth. Let the eggs set, about 1 minute. Break up with a fork. Garnish with chopped scallions (both green and white parts) and cilantro leaves.

sausage, barley, and spinach soup

This quick soup *has it all: flavor from the sausage, texture from the barley, and color (not to mention vitamins) from the spinach.*

1 cup pearl barley

4 cups homemade chicken stock (page 8) or canned low-sodium chicken broth

4 cups water

½ pound chorizo, kielbasa, or other smoked sausage, cut into ¼-inch-thick rounds

10 ounces fresh spinach, washed, tough stems removed, and coarsely chopped

Salt and freshly ground black pepper to taste

1. Combine the barley, chicken stock, water, and sausage in a large saucepan and bring to a boil. Cover, reduce the heat to medium-low, and simmer until the barley is tender, 30 to 35 minutes.

2. Stir in the spinach and simmer until wilted, about 5 minutes. Season with salt and pepper and serve.

makes 6 servings

the simmering bean pot

Simplest Spicy Tomato and Lentil Soup

◆

Lentils in Habanero Oil

◆

Smoky Split Pea Soup

◆

Black Bean Soup with a Shot of Scotch

◆

Black Beans Boiled in Beer

◆

Kidney Beans with Walnut Dressing

◆

Mexican Red Beans with Chipotle Chiles and Cilantro

◆

White Bean Puree

◆

Cannellini and Green Bean Salad with Tarragon Vinaigrette

◆

White Beans with Shrimp

◆

Pasta e Fagioli

◆

continued

Lima Beans with Butter and Herbs

◆

Fava Bean and Watercress Soup

◆

Chickpeas Spanish Style

◆

Spiced Chickpeas and Spinach with Curried Yogurt

Every cuisine has wonderful dried bean recipes, and every one of these recipes calls for rehydrating the beans in simmering water. In this chapter, I've tried to keep it just this simple.

Basically, I either combine plain boiled beans with flavorful dressings to create light salads, or I boil them along with flavoring ingredients for heartier stews or soups. Either way, these one-pot recipes are healthful, interesting, and, above all, easy.

Kidney Beans with Walnut Dressing belongs in the first category. All you do is boil some beans until tender and toss with a "pesto" of ground walnuts, walnut oil, vinegar, garlic, and herbs. Lima Beans with Butter and Herbs is even simpler. Just stir butter and herbs into the warm beans for an earthy but surprisingly luxurious result. Sometimes I'll throw in a crisp, blanched vegetable, as in Cannellini and Green Bean Salad with Tarragon Vinaigrette or Spiced Chickpeas and Spinach with Curried Yogurt, to lighten up the dish.

Black Beans Boiled in Beer falls into the second category. Here the beans are cooked in a mixture of water, beer, vinegar, and spices. When the beans are tender, they're ready to serve in their own delicious sauce. Mexican Red Beans with Chipotle Chiles and Cilantro is likewise cooked in a flavorful mixture— water, garlic, a little brown sugar, and smoky chiles. Either of these recipes is a complete meal when served over white rice or polenta. These beans can also be wrapped in a tortilla with chopped vegetables, rice, and cheese to make a bean burrito, or served as a side dish with chicken, beef, or pork.

Chickpeas Spanish Style is a hybrid recipe. The chickpeas are boiled in water while a flavorful sauce of tomatoes, onions, and saffron is boiled separately. When the two are combined, they make a versatile appetizer, side dish, or vegetarian main course.

While chicken, meat, and vegetable soups really suffer if you don't make them with homemade stock, bean soups shine when you just add water. I've made countless meals of bean soup, salad, and a simple herbed pizza bread (see page 98) and always feel happy and satisfied with the combination. All of the soups in this chapter freeze well, so if you have leftovers, pour them into an airtight container and save for another night.

While cooking beans really is a matter of just adding water, there are a few things you should know for best results:

Common wisdom would have you soak most dried beans overnight or for at least 6 hours before cooking. During the course of my research, however, I saw a number of iconoclastic recipes that suggested skipping the soaking. Since one of my goals in the kitchen is to eliminate every unnecessary step, I tested my recipes without soaking and was pleased with the results. I found that unsoaked beans were equal in flavor and texture to soaked beans. Although soaked beans generally cook 15 to 30 minutes more quickly than unsoaked beans, the convenience of same-day cooking outweighs the slight edge of soaking one day and cooking the next. The "quick soak" method (pouring boiling water over beans and letting them sit for an hour before cooking) actually adds about a half hour to total cooking time since you have to sit around waiting for your beans to soak instead of just putting them in the pot and boiling them up immediately.

Whether you soak or not, cooking beans is easy but not quick. Cooking times for beans vary enormously, but all beans (with the exception of lentils, which take only 15 to 20 minutes) need at least 40 minutes to an hour to become tender. Depending on how old your beans are, they can take much longer. And sometimes, if you've got very stale beans, they'll never soften up, no matter how long you boil them. I buy my beans at a natural foods store where the turnover is quick. This way I'm pretty sure that I'll never wind up with tough, old beans. It's essential to taste your beans often, as soon as you think there's a chance they might be done. Drain them when they are tender but not yet mushy. Properly cooked beans hold their shape but have given up almost all of their crunch. You know you've overcooked them when they start to shed their skins and disintegrate in the water. Try not to let it get that far.

There is also a raging debate about whether or not to add salt to beans as they cook. Some cooks claim that this will prevent the beans from softening. Others say it makes no difference. I am happy to add my salt at the end of cooking. But if you like your beans slightly salty, you might want to add salt halfway through the cooking so that it has time to permeate the beans but won't prevent expedient cooking.

There *is* a piece of common wisdom to which I subscribe. Cooking beans with an acidic ingredient like tomato juice, vinegar, or lemon juice may slow down or completely stall the softening of your beans. Since I like an acidic element in many of my bean dishes, I either keep the amount relatively small or stir it in at the end.

simplest spicy tomato and lentil soup

This is one *of the most flavorful lentil soups I've tasted, owing to the explosive combination of onion, garlic, cilantro, ginger, and spices. Pureeing 1 cup of the soup and adding it back to the pot gives it a smoother consistency, but you can leave out this step if you like.*

1 cup lentils

5 cups water

1 cup canned crushed tomatoes

1 medium-size onion, peeled and finely chopped

4 garlic cloves, peeled and finely chopped

½ cup chopped fresh cilantro leaves

One 1-inch piece fresh gingerroot, finely chopped

1 bay leaf

2 teaspoons sweet paprika

1 teaspoon turmeric

2 tablespoons extra-virgin olive oil

Salt and freshly ground black pepper to taste

1. Sort through the lentils, removing any stones. Rinse and drain in a colander. Combine the lentils, water, tomatoes, onion, garlic, cilantro, ginger, bay leaf, paprika, turmeric, and olive oil in a large saucepan or pot and bring to a boil. Cover, reduce the heat to medium-low, and simmer for 1½ hours. Season with salt and pepper.

2. Puree 1 cup of the soup in a blender or food processor, return to the pot, reheat, and serve.

makes 6 servings

lentils in habanero oil

Habanero chiles, *also known as Scotch Bonnets, are among the hottest in the world. I love their flavor, but they're too spicy to simply mix with lentils. Here, one small chile is steeped in oil and then discarded. The chile oil, mixed with boiled lentils, a little lemon juice, and fresh oregano, gives the dish a subtle (rather than painful) heat.*

1 habanero or other very hot fresh chile

6 tablespoons extra-virgin olive oil

2 cups lentils

1 tablespoon chopped fresh oregano leaves

1 tablespoon fresh lemon juice

Salt to taste

1. Stem the habanero and coarsely chop. Transfer the habanero pieces, with the seeds, to a small bowl, and add the olive oil. Let steep until the oil is hot and spicy, about 1½ hours. Strain the oil into another small bowl, pressing down on the solids with the back of a spoon to extract as much flavor from the chile as possible. Discard the chile pieces and seeds.

2. Sort through the lentils, removing any stones. Rinse and drain in a colander. Place the lentils in a medium-size saucepan and cover with water by at least 1 inch. Bring to a boil, reduce the heat to medium-low, and simmer until tender, 15 to 20 minutes. Drain and transfer to a large bowl.

3. Toss the lentils with the chile oil, oregano, and lemon juice and season with salt. Serve warm, at room temperature, or refrigerate and serve cold.

makes 6 side-dish servings or
4 main-course servings

smoky split pea soup

I used to *sauté the carrots and leeks before adding them to this soup. One day I decided to skip this step—one less pot to wash, 2 tablespoons of butter I didn't need—and I didn't notice any difference in the end result. I still got a classic, thick and smoky soup flecked with bright pink bits of ham and meltingly soft pieces of carrot. I make this in big batches and freeze half. Then, on a cold weeknight, I'll defrost it in the microwave for an instant meal that tastes like it cooked for hours.*

I pound split peas

2½ quarts water

2 smoked ham hocks

2 celery stalks, finely chopped

2 tablespoons finely chopped fresh tarragon leaves

2 medium-size carrots, peeled and finely chopped

2 leeks, white and light green parts, washed and finely chopped

2 tablespoons finely chopped fresh parsley leaves

Salt and freshly ground black pepper to taste

1. Sort through the split peas, removing any stones. Rinse and drain in a colander. Combine the split peas and water in a large saucepan or pot and bring to a boil. Add the ham hocks, celery, and tarragon, reduce the heat to medium-low, and simmer, partially covered, for 45 minutes. Add the carrots and leeks and simmer another 45 minutes.

2. Remove the ham hocks. If the split peas haven't entirely lost their shape, continue to simmer the soup until they do, another 10 to 15 minutes.

3. Take the meat off the ham hock bones, trimming and discarding the visible fat. Shred the meat into small pieces and return to the soup pot. Stir in the parsley, season with salt and pepper, and serve.

makes **8** servings

quickest, best pizza bread

There's nothing like homemade, hot-from-the-oven bread with a bowl of bean soup. But if you're cooking from a book called *Just Add Water*, you probably don't have the time or energy required to produce a perfect baguette at home. Pizza bread is well within your reach, however. Unlike bread dough, pizza dough requires only one short rise. Instead of waiting two hours for your dough to rise and another two hours for it to rise again, your pizza dough is ready to bake in an hour and fifteen minutes. And unlike bread, pizza requires no special skills when it comes to shaping. If your finished pizza looks more like an amoeba than a perfect circle, just explain to everyone that you were going for that rustic, country look. I like to brush my pizza with a little olive oil, salt, maybe a chopped garlic clove, and a tablespoon or two of fresh herbs.

In addition to the bean soups in this chapter, pizza bread makes a meal of other recipes in this book: Curried Cream of Carrot Soup; Butternut Squash Soup; Manhattan Clam Chowder; Saffron Mussel Bisque; Sausage, Barley, and Spinach Soup; Spaghetti and Clams in Hearty Tomato Sauce; Mussels in White Wine over Spaghetti; and Scallops Simmered in Spiced Tomato Broth.

Pizza dough can be frozen in an airtight container after it is punched down. Just defrost on the counter and shape and bake as directed.

1¼ cups warm (not hot) water

I teaspoon active dry yeast

3½ cups all-purpose flour

I teaspoon salt, plus more to taste

3 tablespoons olive oil

I garlic clove (optional), finely chopped

I tablespoon finely chopped fresh herbs
(parsley, basil, oregano, mint, thyme,
sage) (optional)

I. Pour ¼ cup of the warm water into a measuring cup and sprinkle the yeast into the water. Let it stand until the yeast dissolves, 3 to 4 minutes.

2. Combine the flour and I teaspoon salt in the work bowl of a food processor and pulse several times to mix.

3. Add the remaining cup warm water to the measuring cup along with 2 tablespoons of the olive oil. With the motor running, pour the liquid through the feed tube of the food processor. If any yeast remains at the bottom of the cup, scrape it into the tube with a spatula. Process the mixture until it forms a ball, about 30 seconds. Continue to process until smooth, another 30 seconds.

4. Turn the dough into a large bowl and cover the top of the bowl with plastic wrap. Let the dough rise until almost doubled in size, about I hour.

5. Preheat the oven to 500 degrees. Deflate the dough by punching it down and let it rest for 15 minutes. Divide it into two pieces. Shape each one into a rough round by placing it on a floured cookie sheet and patting and pressing it with your fingertips. Combine the remaining tablespoon oil, salt to taste, and the garlic and herbs if desired in a small bowl. Brush the pizzas with the oil mixture, prick the surface all over with a fork, and bake one at a time until golden, 15 to 18 minutes each.

black bean soup with a shot of scotch

Like everyone else, *I always stirred a little sherry into my black bean soup. Then one day I read Joyce Goldstein's suggestion, in her book* Back to Square One, *to substitute scotch whiskey for the sherry. I tried this with my simple soup and was charmed by the result—added warmth and complexity. If you want to make the soup ahead of time, don't add the scotch until the last minute; its flavor dissipates when the soup is reheated. Garnish with dollops of sour cream and a sprinkling of chopped parsley or cilantro, if desired.*

2 cups dried black beans

¼ pound sliced bacon, finely chopped

1 small onion, peeled and finely chopped

3 garlic cloves, peeled and finely chopped

½ teaspoon dried thyme

2 quarts water

Salt and freshly ground black pepper to taste

3 tablespoons scotch whiskey

1. Sort through the beans, removing any stones. Rinse and drain in a colander.

Combine the beans, bacon, onion, garlic, thyme, and water in a large saucepan or pot. Bring to a boil, cover, reduce the heat to medium-low, and simmer until the beans are tender, 1½ to 2 hours. Season with salt and pepper.

2. Puree the soup, in batches if necessary, in a blender. Return to the pot and season again with salt and pepper. Immediately before serving, stir the scotch into the hot soup and ladle into soup bowls.

makes 6 to 8 servings

black beans boiled in beer

Nothing is simpler, *or more satisfying, than a bowl of flavorful black beans over fluffy white rice. Beer is a key ingredient here, as is balsamic vinegar, which gives the beans a slight sweetness. Since the cooking liquid is slightly acidic, these beans take longer to cook than beans simply boiled in water.*

2 cups dried black beans

2 medium-size onions, peeled and finely chopped

2 tablespoons vegetable oil

4 garlic cloves, peeled and finely chopped

I teaspoon chili powder

I teaspoon ground cumin

I teaspoon Tabasco sauce

¼ cup balsamic vinegar

2 cups water

One 12-ounce bottle beer

Salt and freshly ground black pepper to taste

I. Sort through the beans, removing any stones. Rinse and drain in a colander. Combine the onions, vegetable oil, garlic, chili powder, cumin, Tabasco, vinegar, water, and beer in a large saucepan and bring to a simmer.

2. Add the beans, and bring to a simmer again. Cover and cook over low heat until the beans are tender, 3 to 3½ hours. Season with salt and pepper and serve.

makes 6 to 8 side-dish servings or
4 main-course servings

kidney beans with walnut dressing

This recipe *is based on a traditional Eastern European dish. I've lightened it a little by using a smaller amount of walnuts to make a kind of pesto in which the warm beans are tossed. Walnut oil, available in supermarkets and natural food stores, has a wonderful, light flavor that intensifies the flavor of the ground nuts. Serve as a side dish to Boiled Beef with Salsa Verde (page 166) or over rice as a vegetarian main course.*

2 cups dried kidney beans

⅔ cup chopped walnuts

1 garlic clove, peeled

⅔ cup tightly packed fresh cilantro leaves

2 tablespoons red wine vinegar

3 tablespoons walnut oil or extra-virgin olive oil

¼ teaspoon cayenne pepper, or to taste

Salt to taste

1. Sort through the beans, removing any stones. Rinse and drain in a colander. Place the beans in a medium-size saucepan and cover with water. Bring to a boil, cover, reduce the heat to medium-low, and simmer until the beans are soft, 1 to 1½ hours. Reserve ¼ cup of the cooking liquid. Drain the beans in a colander and place in a medium-size bowl.

2. While the beans are cooking, prepare the dressing. Combine the walnuts, garlic, and cilantro in the work bowl of a food processor. Pulse several times to

finely chop (but not grind) the nuts. Scrape the mixture into a small bowl and stir in the vinegar, walnut oil, cayenne, and salt. Add 2 tablespoons of the reserved bean cooking water to thin the dressing. Stir the dressing into the beans. If the mixture looks a little dry, stir another tablespoon or two of the reserved water into the beans. Serve warm, at room temperature, or refrigerate up to 24 hours and bring to room temperature before serving.

makes 6 side-dish servings or
4 main-course servings

mexican red beans with chipotle chiles and cilantro

Canned chipotle chiles, *available in Latin groceries and many supermarkets, have an unusual, smoky flavor and a subtle spiciness. They're a great convenience because, unlike dried chiles, they're ready to use right from the can. Two medium-size chipotles give these beans some good heat. If you like a milder dish, use just one. If you are a real hothead, use more to taste.*

2 cups dried red kidney or pinto beans

I medium-size onion, peeled and finely chopped

2 tablespoons vegetable oil

4 garlic cloves, peeled and finely chopped

2 canned chipotle chiles in adobo, finely chopped, or more or less to taste

2 tablespoons adobo sauce from the can

I tablespoon firmly packed brown sugar

I teaspoon ground cumin

4 cups water

2 tablespoons fresh lime juice

¼ cup finely chopped fresh cilantro leaves

Salt and freshly ground black pepper to taste

I. Sort through the beans, removing any stones. Rinse and drain in a colander. Combine the onion, vegetable oil, garlic, chiles, adobo sauce, brown sugar, cumin, and water in a large saucepan and bring to a simmer. Add the beans and bring to a simmer again. Cover and cook at a bare simmer over low heat until the beans are tender, 2½ to 3 hours.

2. Stir in the lime juice and cilantro, season with salt and pepper, and serve.

makes 6 side-dish servings or
4 main-course servings

white bean puree

This is a *great all-purpose side-dish recipe. It makes a nice change from rice or mashed potatoes when you're serving a simple roast chicken or grilled fish. It's especially good with a main course like Hearty Beef Stew (page 165) or Braised Pork Roast with Yams (page 176), since it acts as a sponge for all the delicious stew juices. A little added nutmeg gives these beans a subtle spice, but is optional. So is olive oil, for drizzling.*

2 cups dried navy or cannellini beans

1 bay leaf

4 garlic cloves, peeled and crushed

4 fresh thyme sprigs

2 quarts water

¼ cup extra-virgin olive oil, plus more for drizzling, if desired

⅛ teaspoon ground nutmeg (optional)

Salt and freshly ground black pepper to taste

1. Sort through the beans, removing any stones. Rinse and drain in a colander.

Combine the beans, bay leaf, garlic, thyme, and water in a large saucepan and bring to a boil. Reduce the heat to medium-low and simmer, partially covered, until the beans are soft, 1½ to 2 hours. Reserve 1 cup of the cooking liquid. Drain the beans and discard the bay leaf and thyme.

2. Transfer the beans to the work bowl of a food processor. With the motor running, add the olive oil, then add the reserved bean cooking water in a slow stream until the beans are smooth and creamy. They should be the consistency

of very soft, fluffy mashed potatoes. Stir in the nutmeg if desired, season with salt and pepper, and serve warm. The bean puree may be made several hours in advance, refrigerated in an airtight container, and reheated in the microwave. Serve with additional olive oil on the side for drizzling, if desired.

makes 4 servings

bean dips

A cup or two of boiled beans can quickly become a party dip or sandwich spread with the addition of a few flavoring ingredients and a quick whirl in the food processor. I usually add ¼ cup of liquid (citrus juice, oil, water, yogurt, sour cream) to the beans for smoothness, but you may need more or less depending on the consistency and water content of your cooked beans. As for flavor combinations, the only limit is your imagination. Here are a few that I like:

Lemony White Bean Dip: Combine 2 cups any cooked white navy or kidney beans, 1 peeled garlic clove, 1 cup tightly packed fresh parsley leaves, ¼ cup fresh lemon juice, and ¼ cup extra-virgin olive oil in the work bowl of a food processor and process until smooth. Season with salt and pepper.

White Bean and Anchovy Dip: Combine 2 cups any cooked white navy or kidney beans, 1 peeled garlic clove, ½ cup tightly packed fresh parsley leaves, 2 tablespoons fresh lemon juice, ¼ cup extra-virgin olive oil, and 2 coarsely chopped anchovies in the work bowl of a food processor and process until smooth. Stir in 1 tablespoon coarsely chopped capers and season with salt and pepper.

Hummus: Combine 2 cups cooked chickpeas, 1 peeled garlic clove, ½ cup tahini (sesame paste available at natural food stores and in many supermarkets), ¼ cup fresh lemon juice, and ½ teaspoon sweet paprika in the work bowl of a food processor and process until smooth. Season with salt and pepper.

Chickpea and Cumin Dip: Combine 2 cups cooked chickpeas, 1 peeled garlic clove, ½ teaspoon ground cumin, ½ cup tightly packed fresh mint leaves, 1 tablespoon fresh lime juice, and ½ cup plain yogurt in the work bowl of a food processor and process until smooth. Season with salt and pepper.

Chickpea and Sun-Dried Tomato Dip: Combine 2 cups cooked chickpeas, 6 coarsely chopped sun-dried tomatoes packed in oil, ½ cup tightly packed fresh basil leaves, 1 tablespoon red wine vinegar, and ¼ cup extra-virgin olive oil in the work bowl of a food processor and process until smooth. Stir in 2 tablespoons finely chopped black olives and season with salt and pepper.

Yellow Split Pea Dip: Combine 2 cups cooked yellow split peas, ¼ cup tightly packed fresh oregano leaves, 1 peeled garlic clove, ½ cup plain yogurt, and ½ teaspoon grated lemon zest in the work bowl of a food processor and process until smooth. Season with salt and pepper.

Spicy Black Bean Dip: Combine 2 cups cooked black beans, 1 seeded jalapeño chile, ½ cup tightly packed fresh cilantro leaves, ½ cup sour cream or plain yogurt, and ½ teaspoon chili powder in the work bowl of a food processor and process until smooth. Scrape into a bowl and stir in 1 finely chopped small plum tomato and 2 finely chopped scallions, white and green parts. Season with salt and pepper.

cannellini and green bean salad with tarragon vinaigrette

This combination of *dried and fresh beans makes a substantial, fresh-tasting salad. Preparation is especially simple since the green beans are blanched in the same pot as the cannellini beans. Serve it as a side dish with simply grilled fish or meat or serve it on its own as a vegetarian main course.*

1 cup dried cannellini or other white beans

1½ quarts water

¼ pound fresh green beans, ends trimmed

1 ripe plum tomato, cut into ¼-inch dice

1 tablespoon finely chopped red onion

1 teaspoon finely chopped fresh tarragon
   leaves

1 tablespoon tarragon vinegar

2 tablespoons extra-virgin olive oil

1 teaspoon Dijon mustard

Salt and freshly ground black pepper to taste

1. Sort through the beans, removing any stones. Rinse and drain in a colander. Combine the cannellini beans and water in a large saucepan and bring to a boil. Cover, reduce the heat to medium-low and simmer until just tender, 1 to 1½ hours. Add the green beans to the pot and simmer until just tender, 2 to 3 minutes. Drain the beans and place them in a large bowl.

2. Combine the tomato, onion, tarragon, vinegar, olive oil, mustard, salt, and pepper in a small bowl. Pour the

dressing over the beans and mix well.
Season with salt and pepper. Serve
immediately or refrigerate up to 3 hours
and bring to room temperature before
serving.

makes 6 side-dish servings or
4 main-course servings

white beans with shrimp

White beans *become a creamy background for boiled shrimp. A bracing dressing spiked with anchovies and herbs enlivens the combination. Beans also add bulk to the dish, stretching a half pound of shrimp to serve as many as six.*

1 cup dried navy or cannellini beans

2 teaspoons salt, plus more to taste

½ pound medium-size shrimp

1 small ripe plum tomato, cut into ¼-inch dice

2 tablespoons finely chopped fresh herbs (parsley, basil, mint, oregano)

¼ cup extra-virgin olive oil

2 tablespoons fresh lemon juice

1 anchovy fillet, finely chopped

Salt and freshly ground black pepper to taste

Romaine lettuce leaves for garnish (optional)

1. Sort through the beans, removing any stones. Rinse and drain in a colander. Place the beans in a medium-size saucepan, cover with water, and bring to a boil. Cover, reduce the heat to medium-low, and simmer until the beans are soft, 1 to 1½ hours. Drain the beans in a colander and place in a medium-size bowl.

2. While the beans are cooking, prepare the shrimp. Bring a large saucepan of water to boil. Add the salt and shrimp and cook until pink, 1 to 2 minutes. Drain, cool slightly, peel, and coarsely chop.

3. Add the chopped shrimp, tomato, herbs, olive oil, lemon juice, and anchovy to the beans and season with salt and pepper. Stir to combine. Serve immediately on top of lettuce if desired, or refrigerate up to 6 hours and let come to room temperature before serving.

makes 4 to 6 appetizer servings or
2 to 3 main-course servings

pasta e fagioli

I use a *tiny pasta shape so that I can cook the pasta quickly right in the soup. White beans are traditional, but chickpeas, kidney beans, or lima beans are just as good.*

1½ cups dried navy or cannellini beans

2 quarts water

4 garlic cloves, peeled and thinly sliced

1 medium-size onion, peeled

2 bay leaves

2 sprigs fresh rosemary

1 cup orzo or pastina

1 cup canned crushed tomatoes

1 teaspoon salt, plus more to taste

¼ cup finely chopped fresh basil leaves

Freshly ground black pepper to taste

¼ cup extra-virgin olive oil

Freshly grated Parmesan cheese

1. Sort through the beans, removing any stones. Rinse and drain in a colander. Combine the beans, water, garlic, onion, bay leaves, and rosemary in a large saucepan or pot. Bring to a boil, reduce the heat to medium-low, and simmer, covered, until the beans are tender, 1 to 1½ hours. Remove and discard the onion, bay leaves, and rosemary.

2. Turn the heat to medium-high and add the orzo or pastina, tomatoes, and salt. Cook at a lively simmer until the orzo is just tender, 7 to 10 minutes. If the soup is too thick, stir in ½ to 1 cup more water and heat through. Stir in the basil and season with salt and pepper. Ladle the soup into bowls and drizzle with the olive oil. Serve with the grated Parmesan cheese on the side.

makes 6 servings

lima beans with butter and herbs

Sometimes *the simplest preparations are the best. Here lowly lima beans are cooked until tender, then tossed with butter and herbs to create a surprisingly luxurious side dish.*

1 cup dried lima or baby lima beans

1½ quarts water

1 bay leaf

1 small onion, peeled and quartered

1 garlic clove, peeled and crushed

2 tablespoons unsalted butter, cut into several pieces

2 tablespoons finely chopped mixed fresh herbs (basil, parsley, oregano, mint, chives)

Salt and freshly ground black pepper to taste

1. Sort through the beans, removing any stones. Rinse and drain in a colander.

Combine the beans, water, bay leaf, onion, and garlic in a large saucepan and bring to a boil. Cover, reduce the heat to medium-low, and simmer until the beans are tender, 45 minutes to 1 hour.

2. Drain the beans in a colander and discard the bay leaf, onion, and garlic. Transfer the beans to a medium-size serving bowl and toss with the butter, herbs, salt, and pepper. Serve warm.

makes 4 to 6 servings

fava bean and watercress soup

Fava beans *make a rich but low-fat soup. Drizzling a little of the very best olive oil over each bowl is an optional luxury, as is shaving a few curls of best-quality Parmesan cheese over each bowl (do this with a vegetable peeler). Peeled and split fava beans can be found in natural foods stores and Middle Eastern groceries. Dried lima beans may be substituted if favas are unavailable.*

1 pound peeled and split dried fava beans

2 quarts water

1 medium-size onion, peeled and finely chopped

4 celery stalks, finely chopped

4 garlic cloves, peeled and finely chopped

1 bay leaf

Salt and freshly ground black pepper to taste

1 bunch watercress, washed, stems removed, and leaves coarsely chopped

⅓ cup extra-virgin olive oil (optional)

Parmesan cheese for garnish, sliced into curls with a vegetable peeler (optional)

1. Sort through the beans, removing any stones. Rinse and drain in a colander. Combine the beans, water, onion, celery, garlic, and bay leaf in a large saucepan or pot and bring to a boil. Reduce the heat to low, cover, and simmer until the beans are tender, 45 minutes to 1 hour.

2. Puree the soup in a blender, in batches if necessary, and return to the pot. Season with salt and pepper. Stir in the watercress and simmer until wilted, 2 to 3 minutes. Ladle the soup into bowls; drizzle with the olive oil and garnish with Parmesan curls, if desired.

makes 6 to 8 servings

chickpeas spanish style

This dish *is based on a popular tapas bar item, thus the name. It can be served as part of a larger tapas or antipasto spread, or as a side dish with chicken, fish, or meat. Chickpeas are cooked separately here and added to a sauce of sliced onions slowly simmered in tomato sauce. Add a pinch of saffron if you like a more intense flavor.*

1½ cups dried chickpeas

2 garlic cloves, peeled

I bay leaf

4 cups plus 2 tablespoons water

2 tablespoons extra-virgin olive oil

I medium-size onion, peeled and thinly sliced

½ cup canned crushed tomatoes

Pinch of saffron threads (optional), crushed

½ teaspoon salt, plus more to taste

Freshly ground black pepper to taste

I. Sort through the beans, removing any stones. Rinse and drain in a colander. Combine the chickpeas, garlic, bay leaf, and 4 cups of the water in a large saucepan or pot and bring to a boil. Cover, reduce the heat to medium-low, and simmer until the beans are soft, I to 1½ hours. Drain the beans in a colander, discard the bay leaf and garlic, and set aside.

2. Combine the remaining 2 tablespoons water, the olive oil, onion, tomatoes, saffron if desired, and salt in a small saucepan and bring to a boil. Reduce the heat to low, cover, and cook at a bare simmer until the onion is very soft, about 20 minutes. Stir in the chickpeas, season with salt and pepper, and cook until heated through, 2 to 3 minutes.

makes 4 servings

spiced chickpeas and spinach with curried yogurt

Chickpeas *are cooked in a big pot of water, and then the spinach is added for a minute at the end to quickly blanch it. The combination is then seasoned with garam masala, a blend of cumin, cinnamon, pepper, cloves, coriander, and cardamom, available at gourmet shops and in the spice section of many supermarkets. Curried yogurt adds another dimension of flavor and texture. Serve with warm pita breads for an unusual one-dish meal.*

2 cups dried chickpeas

4 quarts water

2 garlic cloves, peeled

I bay leaf

I pound spinach, washed, tough stems removed, and leaves coarsely chopped

2 tablespoons neutral-tasting vegetable oil, such as canola

I tablespoon fresh lime juice

I teaspoon garam masala

I jalapeño chile, seeded and finely chopped (optional)

Salt

2 cups plain low-fat yogurt

I tablespoon curry powder

2 tablespoons chopped fresh cilantro leaves

I. Sort through the beans, removing any stones. Rinse and drain in a colander. Combine the chickpeas, water, garlic, and bay leaf in a large saucepan or pot and bring to a boil. Cover, reduce the heat to medium-low, and simmer until tender, I to I½ hours. Stir the spinach

into the pot and cook until wilted, about
1 minute. Drain the chickpeas and
spinach, discard the garlic and bay leaf,
and place in a large serving bowl. Toss
with the vegetable oil, lime juice, garam
masala, jalapeño if desired, and salt to
taste.

2. Combine the yogurt, curry powder,
and cilantro in a medium-size bowl and
serve on the side with the chickpeas.

makes 4 servings

express grains

Fusilli with Raw Tomato-Avocado Sauce

◆

Egg Noodles with Indonesian Peanut Sauce

◆

Quickest Fettuccine with Mascarpone and Asparagus

◆

Spaghetti alla Carbonara

◆

Old-fashioned Macaroni and Cheese

◆

Orzo with Prosciutto and Peas

◆

Couscous with Dried Apricots and Pistachios

◆

Couscous with Black Olives and Orange Zest

◆

Coconut Rice with Scallions and Peanuts

◆

Rice Salad with Cucumber and Dill

◆

Sesame Rice Salad with Asparagus

◆

Boiled Arborio Rice with Arugula and Mozzarella Strands

◆

continued

Boiled Arborio Rice with Lemon and Parmesan

♦

Boiled Arborio Rice with Smoked Salmon and Capers

♦

Polenta with Three Cheeses

♦

Polenta with Fresh Corn and Chives

♦

Polenta with Swiss Chard and Simmered Tomato Sauce

♦

Pearl Barley with Sunflower Seeds and Dried Cherries

♦

Pearl Barley and Pesto

♦

Pearl Barley, Porcini, and Parmesan

♦

Bulgur with Spinach and Cashews

♦

Bulgur and Carrots with Cumin-Coriander Dressing

♦

Walnut-Tarragon Quinoa

♦

Quinoa with Prosciutto, Figs, and Mint

Even novices and infrequent cooks feel comfortable boiling pasta. Get over your anxiety about what exactly *al dente* means (it means a little firm to the bite, by the way), and what's to worry about? You throw the pasta in the water and drain it a few minutes later. Cooking rice is just a variation on this theme—except that, in most cases, you don't even have to drain the rice. Less common grains—polenta, bulgur, barley, quinoa—are just as user-friendly (see Grain Glossary, page 125). Even if you've never made them before, rest assured that they're among the simplest, most nourishing foods any water-boiler can prepare. I've kept the following recipes as streamlined as possible. There are no time-consuming sauces or difficult-to-prepare vegetable accompaniments, no sautéing, toasting, baking, or roasting to complicate the basically simple cooking of grains.

Salads are among the easiest and freshest-tasting ways to enjoy grains. Boiled grains are tossed with chopped vegetables and herbs and a simple dressing to make a side dish or a one-dish meal. They can be as humble as Rice Salad with Dill and Cucumber, as exotic as Bulgur and Carrots with Cumin-Coriander Dressing, or as luxurious as Quinoa with Pro-sciutto, Figs, and Mint. Once you learn the ratio of grain to dressing, it is easy enough to devise combinations of your own.

In some of the recipes below, the heat from the just-cooked grain warms ingredients added immediately before serving. Pesto over pasta might seem ho-hum by now, but stirred into piping-hot pearl barley it is wonderfully different. Boiled Arborio Rice with Arugula and Mozzarella Strands is a creamy delight without all the stirring that true risotto requires. Warm your plates or bowls for 10 minutes in a 200-degree oven before spooning out these dishes, since they tend to cool off quickly without this precaution.

Whenever possible, I like to take advantage of the fact that I'm already boiling water by cooking a vegetable in the same pot with the grain. For Sesame Rice Salad with Asparagus, the asparagus is quickly steamed in the hot cooked rice. The peas for Orzo with Prosciutto and Peas are thrown into the pot with the almost-cooked orzo and the two ingredients are drained together before being tossed with prosciutto and a little cheese. Swiss chard stirred into hot polenta quickly wilts; the combination is then topped with a simmered tomato sauce for a rustic vegetarian main course. For an Indian-inspired grain and vegetable dish, spinach is cooked in the water that is then used to rehydrate bulgur. When cooking grains, you can't beat this sort of doubling up for ease and variety.

grain glossary

Here's a brief guide to the grains used in this chapter. Pasta, couscous, rice, and barley are all available in supermarkets. If your market doesn't carry Arborio rice or polenta (most do), go to an Italian grocery. If your market doesn't have bulgur or quinoa (again, most do), check a natural foods store.

Arborio rice: A medium-grain white rice imported from Italy, Arborio rice has more starch than long-grain rice, which accounts for its creamy texture when cooked. Risotto is Arborio rice that is stirred constantly as hot liquid is slowly poured into the pot. But Arborio rice can also be boiled, drained in a colander, and tossed with cheese, butter, and other flavoring ingredients for a less laborious but equally luxurious dish.

Bulgur: Wheat berries that have been steamed, dried, and cracked make bulgur. Because bulgur has already been cooked, it simply needs to be rehydrated with boiling water before serving. Its whole wheat flavor and fine texture make bulgur a hearty yet surprisingly delicate base for all kinds of salads.

Couscous: A tiny wheat pasta used in North African cooking, couscous has become popular here because it's versatile and simple to prepare. Just add it to boiling water, cover, remove from the heat, and let stand for five minutes before dressing and serving. Couscous provides heft and a neutral background for all kinds of ingredients, from steamed vegetables to meat, poultry, and seafood.

Long-grain rice: Long-grain white rice is fluffy, with grains that don't stick together. It cooks up in 20 minutes or less. Long-grain brown rice hasn't had its bran and germ removed. This makes it more nutritious and higher in fiber but also gives it a longer cooking time. If you substitute brown rice for white, be aware that it takes about twice as long to cook.

Pasta: Dried pasta, made of durum wheat and water, comes in many shapes and sizes. Choose a shape that matches your sauce. Orzo, a tiny rice-shaped pasta, works with similarly small peas and pieces of prosciutto. The twists of fusilli help trap bits of tomato and avocado. Sometimes fresh pasta, made with eggs and flour, is an appropriate choice for a rich sauce— Indonesian peanut sauce or mascarpone and fresh asparagus, for example. Avoid the "fresh" pasta found in the refrigerator case of the supermarket. It's never as fresh tasting and tender as it should be. Seek out fresh egg pasta sold at pasta shops or Asian groceries, since it's usually fresher and of better quality.

Pearl barley: This nutty grain is larger than rice and has a substantial but not heavy texture. Barley takes about 30 minutes to cook. It can be used in place of rice when you want something a little bit chewy and earthy.

Polenta: Polenta is simply the Italian name for cornmeal. When preparing traditional polenta recipes, cornmeal is poured into boiling water and stirred constantly for about half an hour, until stiff. Instant polenta, called for in the recipes below, has been cooked and then dried, so that it only has to be rehydrated and heated through for several minutes before it's ready to eat. Polenta is a quintessential comfort food, whether it is served as a savory side dish with fresh corn and chives stirred in, or dished up for breakfast with maple syrup and a pat of butter melting on top.

Quinoa: An ancient grain originally cultivated by the Incas, quinoa has tiny grains with a light, crunchy texture. Quinoa is a real super-food, high in protein and nutrients. Use it as you would rice or bulgur.

fusilli with raw tomato-avocado sauce

The addition of *avocado to a quick no-cook tomato sauce makes this pasta dish a little bit different. To prevent the avocado from turning brown, sprinkle with lemon juice immediately after you chop it.*

4 medium-size ripe tomatoes (about 1½ pounds), cut into ½-inch dice

2 garlic cloves, peeled and finely chopped

2 tablespoons capers, finely chopped

2 tablespoons finely chopped fresh oregano leaves

3 tablespoons extra-virgin olive oil

1½ teaspoons salt

¼ teaspoon hot red pepper flakes

1 medium-size ripe avocado

2 tablespoons fresh lemon juice

1 pound fusilli or other curly pasta shape

1. Combine the tomatoes, garlic, capers, oregano, olive oil, ½ teaspoon of the salt, and the red pepper flakes in a large bowl. Peel the avocado, pit it, and cut into ¼-inch dice. Place in a small bowl and sprinkle with the lemon juice.

2. Bring a large pot of water to boil. Add the remaining teaspoon salt and the fusilli and cook until tender. Drain and toss with the tomato mixture. Divide the pasta among four pasta bowls and spoon some avocado over each bowl. Serve immediately.

makes 4 servings

egg noodles with indonesian peanut sauce

I always *have the ingredients for this no-cook pasta sauce on hand in my pantry, so it's become an old standby on busy nights when I haven't been to the market. If I do have time, I pop into the local Asian grocery for some fresh egg noodles.*

½ cup smooth peanut butter

1 tablespoon Asian sesame oil

2 tablespoons soy sauce

2 tablespoons fresh lemon juice

¼ cup water

1 small garlic clove, peeled

½ teaspoon hot red pepper flakes, or to taste

1 teaspoon sugar

1 pound fresh Asian egg noodles or spaghetti

1 tablespoon salt

6 scallions, white and light green parts, finely chopped

1 cucumber, peeled, seeded, and cut into ¼-inch dice

1. Combine the peanut butter, sesame oil, soy sauce, lemon juice, water, garlic, red pepper flakes, and sugar in the work bowl of a food processor or blender and process until smooth. The sauce can be made up to 6 hours before serving and stored at room temperature.

2. Bring a large pot of water to boil. Add the noodles and salt and cook until tender. Drain and toss the noodles with the sauce, scallions, and cucumber in a large serving bowl. Serve immediately, or refrigerate and serve cold or at room temperature.

makes 4 servings

quickest fettuccine with mascarpone and asparagus

I avoid *"fresh" pasta that's packaged in plastic and sold in the supermarket. It just doesn't have the taste and tenderness of fresh homemade pasta. Buy fresh pasta from an Italian deli or pasta shop; otherwise, use imported dried noodles. Heat your pasta bowls for 5 or 10 minutes in an oven set at the lowest heat possible to ensure that your food remains hot as you eat it.*

¾ **cup mascarpone, at room temperature**

½ **cup freshly grated Parmesan cheese**

¼ **cup finely chopped fresh mint leaves**

¼ **cup finely chopped fresh basil leaves**

Salt and freshly ground black pepper to taste

1½ **pounds fresh or 1 pound dried fettuccine**

1 **pound asparagus, ends trimmed and cut into 1-inch lengths**

1. Combine the mascarpone, Parmesan, mint, basil, salt, and pepper in a small bowl.

2. Bring a large pot of water to boil. Add the fettuccine and 1 tablespoon salt and cook until just tender. Add the asparagus to the pot and cook for 1 minute. Reserve ¼ cup of the cooking liquid and drain the pasta and asparagus.

3. Return the pasta and asparagus to the hot pot and stir in the cheese mixture. Add the reserved hot cooking liquid 1 tablespoon at a time until the pasta is creamy but not too wet. Adjust the salt and pepper if necessary. Divide the pasta among four warm bowls and serve immediately.

makes 4 servings

spaghetti alla carbonara

Most recipes *for* spaghetti alla carbonara *call for frying bacon or pancetta, but this one, adapted from Elizabeth Luard's* Old World Kitchen, *is much simpler. Just boil the spaghetti and toss with the rest of the ingredients. The eggs cook on contact with the hot pasta. Warm the bowls before serving so that your dinner doesn't cool off too quickly while you eat it.*

I garlic clove, peeled and finely chopped

3 tablespoons extra-virgin olive oil

I tablespoon salt

I pound spaghetti

2 large eggs, lightly beaten

½ cup freshly grated Parmesan cheese, plus more for serving

¼ pound sliced prosciutto, finely chopped

½ teaspoon grated lemon zest

2 tablespoons chopped fresh parsley leaves

Freshly ground black pepper to taste

I. Combine the garlic and olive oil in a small bowl and set aside. Bring a large pot of water to boil. Add the spaghetti and salt and cook until just tender.

2. Reserve ¼ cup of the cooking liquid, then drain the spaghetti and return it to the hot pot. Pour in the beaten eggs and stir until well combined. Stir in the garlic oil, cheese, prosciutto, lemon zest, parsley, salt, and abundant black pepper until well combined. If the pasta looks dry, stir in the reserved cooking liquid I tablespoon at a time until it's creamy but not watery. Serve immediately in warm pasta bowls.

makes 4 servings

Note: Raw eggs should not be used in food to be consumed by children, pregnant women, or anyone in poor health or with a compromised immune system because of the danger of salmonella. Make sure you buy the freshest eggs possible.

old-fashioned macaroni and cheese

This is the *ultimate version of everyone's childhood favorite. Its relation to the packaged variety is as a Valhrona chocolate cake is to a Hershey bar. The crumbled crackers help cut the richness of the macaroni and are in keeping with the humble character of the dish. Gruyère or Jack cheese may be substituted for Cheddar. Some cheeses are quite salty, so taste before seasoning.*

2 large eggs

One 12-ounce can evaporated milk

¼ teaspoon Tabasco sauce

1 teaspoon dry mustard

¾ pound elbow macaroni

1 teaspoon salt, plus more to taste

¼ cup (½ stick) unsalted butter

12 ounces sharp Cheddar, grated (about 3 cups)

10 saltine crackers, coarsely crumbled

1. Whisk together the eggs, 1 cup of the milk, the Tabasco, and mustard in a small bowl and set aside.

2. Bring a large saucepan of water to boil. Add the macaroni and salt. Cook until almost tender (you want the macaroni to be a minute or two from being cooked so that it doesn't get mushy when cooked again). Drain, return to the pot, and toss with the butter over low heat until melted.

3. Add the egg mixture and about three-quarters of the cheese to the macaroni and stir until the cheese is melted. Constantly stirring, slowly add the remaining ½ cup milk and the remaining cheese. Continue to stir until creamy and piping hot, about 5 minutes. Season with salt, if necessary. Spoon into four bowls and top with cracker crumbs. Serve immediately.

makes 4 servings

orzo with prosciutto and peas

This dish showcases *the best of Italy—pasta, prosciutto, and Parmesan. Green peas add fresh flavor and color. A little butter moistens the mixture. I love this as a main course with a green salad before or after, but it would also be a nice first course or accompaniment to a more elaborate meal of roast chicken or broiled fish.*

1 pound orzo

1 tablespoon salt, plus more to taste

1 cup shelled fresh or frozen peas

2 ounces sliced prosciutto, finely chopped

½ cup freshly grated Parmesan cheese

2 tablespoons unsalted butter

Freshly ground black pepper to taste

I. Bring a large pot of water to boil. Add the orzo and salt and cook until the orzo is just tender. Add the peas and cook 30 seconds.

2. Drain the orzo and peas in a colander and return to the hot pot. Toss with the prosciutto, Parmesan, and butter, season with salt and pepper, and serve immediately.

makes 4 servings

couscous with dried apricots and pistachios

This easy dish *is wonderful with chicken or lamb kebabs. I like pistachios for their color and flavor, but any other nuts you have on hand would work well.*

2¼ cups water

One 10-ounce box instant couscous

½ teaspoon salt

6 tablespoons extra-virgin olive oil

½ cup shelled pistachio nuts,
    coarsely chopped

½ cup dried apricots, coarsely chopped

1 teaspoon grated lemon zest

2 tablespoons chopped fresh parsley leaves

2 tablespoons ground cumin

3 tablespoons fresh lemon juice

Freshly ground black pepper to taste

1. Bring the water to boil in a medium-size saucepan. Stir in the couscous, salt, and 1 tablespoon of the olive oil. Remove the pan from the heat and cover. Let stand for 5 minutes and fluff with a fork.

2. Transfer the couscous to a large serving bowl. Stir in the remaining ingredients (including the remaining 5 tablespoons oil) and serve warm or refrigerate and serve cold.

makes 4 servings

couscous with black olives and orange zest

Serve this side dish *when you crave something with bold flavors. It's especially good with seafood and grilled chicken.*

6 tablespoons extra-virgin olive oil

2 tablespoons sherry wine vinegar

½ cup black olives, pitted and coarsely chopped

2 teaspoons grated orange zest

I small garlic clove, peeled and finely chopped

I¼ cups homemade chicken stock (page 8) or canned low-sodium chicken broth

I cup water

One 10-ounce box instant couscous

½ teaspoon salt

Freshly ground black pepper to taste

2 tablespoons chopped fresh parsley leaves

I· Combine 5 tablespoons of the olive oil, the vinegar, olives, orange zest, and garlic in a small bowl. Let stand at room temperature for half an hour or up to I day.

2· Bring the chicken stock and water to boil in a medium-size saucepan. Stir in the couscous, salt, and remaining tablespoon olive oil. Remove the pan from the heat and cover. Let stand for 5 minutes and fluff with a fork.

3· Transfer the couscous to a large serving bowl. Stir in the dressing, pepper, and parsley. Serve warm or refrigerate and serve cold.

makes 4 servings

coconut rice with scallions and peanuts

Bright yellow *because of the turmeric, creamy and a little bit sweet from the coconut milk, this side dish adds color and richness to a meal of grilled chicken breasts or a meaty fish like swordfish or tuna. Add ¾ pound of small cooked, peeled shrimp and it becomes an irresistible main dish on its own.*

I cup unsweetened coconut milk

I cup water

I cup long-grain white rice

¼ teaspoon turmeric (available in any supermarket)

¼ teaspoon ground coriander

I jalapeño or other small hot chile (optional), seeded and finely chopped

½ teaspoon salt, plus more to taste

4 scallions, white and light green parts, finely chopped

¼ cup roasted peanuts, coarsely chopped

I. Combine the coconut milk, water, rice, turmeric, coriander, jalapeño (if using) and salt in a medium-size saucepan. Bring to a boil, reduce the heat to medium-low, cover, and simmer until all the liquid is absorbed and the rice is tender, 18 to 20 minutes.

2. Stir in the scallions and peanuts, adjust the salt, and serve.

makes 4 servings

rice salad with cucumber and dill

Dry mustard *adds kick to this soothing combination of rice, cucumber, and dill. Depending on freshness, mustard can be explosively hot or very mild, so taste and season accordingly. For an Asian-flavored variation, substitute 1 tablespoon Asian sesame oil for 1 tablespoon of the olive oil, wasabi powder for the mustard, and cilantro for the dill, and add 1 teaspoon soy sauce. Either way, serve with broiled, grilled, or poached fish or seafood.*

1½ cups long-grain white rice

2¼ cups water

½ teaspoon salt

3 tablespoons extra-virgin olive oil

2 tablespoons fresh lemon juice

I teaspoon dry mustard, or more to taste

I cucumber, peeled, seeded, and cut into ¼-inch dice

2 tablespoons finely chopped fresh dill

Freshly ground black pepper to taste

I. Combine the rice, water, and salt in a medium-size saucepan. Bring to a boil, reduce the heat to medium-low, cover, and simmer until most of the liquid is absorbed, 18 to 20 minutes.

2. In a small bowl, whisk together the olive oil, lemon, juice, and mustard. Stir the dressing, cucumber, and dill into the rice and season with salt and pepper. Refrigerate until ready to serve.

makes 4 servings

sesame rice salad with asparagus

A dish *to please efficiency experts, since the rice and asparagus are cooked in one pot. Serve with Asian-marinated flank steak, fish, or shrimp.*

1½ cups long-grain white rice

2¼ cups water

½ teaspoon salt

¾ pound asparagus, bottoms trimmed and cut into 1-inch lengths

2 tablespoons Asian sesame oil

2 tablespoons rice wine vinegar

1½ tablespoons soy sauce

1 tablespoon sugar

2 scallions, white and green parts, finely chopped

2 tablespoons finely chopped fresh cilantro leaves

2 tablespoons toasted (see Note) sesame seeds for garnish (optional)

1. Combine the rice, water, and salt in a medium-size saucepan. Bring to a boil, reduce the heat to medium-low, cover, and simmer until most of the liquid is absorbed, 15 to 18 minutes. Stir in the asparagus, cover, and cook until the rice is cooked and the asparagus tender, another 2 to 3 minutes. Transfer the cooked rice and asparagus to a serving bowl.

2. In a small bowl, whisk together the sesame oil, vinegar, soy sauce, and sugar. Stir the dressing, scallions, and cilantro into the rice and season with salt. Refrigerate until ready to serve. Garnish with the sesame seeds if desired.

Note: To toast sesame seeds, place in a small skillet over low heat and cook, stirring frequently, until golden, 3 to 4 minutes.

makes 4 servings

instant main-course salads

Many side-dish recipes in this chapter instantly become main courses with the addition of some poached chicken, shrimp, or chopped deli ham or turkey. Simplify your life by making one of these one-dish meals:

- Shred 1 poached whole boneless chicken breast (page 10) and add to: Coconut Rice with Scallions and Peanuts; Sesame Rice Salad with Asparagus; Rice Salad with Cucumber and Dill; Couscous with Dried Apricots and Pistachios; Egg Noodles with Indonesian Peanut Sauce; or Bulgur with Spinach and Cashews.

- Add ½ pound cooked peeled shrimp to: Coconut Rice with Scallions and Peanuts; Sesame Rice Salad with Asparagus; Rice Salad with Cucumber and Dill; or Egg Noodles with Indonesian Peanut Sauce.

- Add 2 to 3 ounces (½ to ¾ cup) diced ham to: Rice Salad with Cucumber and Dill or Couscous with Black Olives and Orange Zest.

- Add 2 to 3 ounces (½ to ¾ cup) diced turkey to: Couscous with Dried Apricots and Pistachios; Pearl Barley with Sunflower Seeds and Dried Cherries; or Walnut-Tarragon Quinoa.

boiled arborio rice with arugula and mozzarella strands

Arborio rice, *imported from Italy, is usually used in risotto recipes, but it can also simply be boiled and then mixed with a variety of flavorful ingredients. You get the same creamy rice, but there's no stirring and no difficult cleanup (if you've ever had to take on a dirty risotto pot with a battery of Brillo pads you know what I mean). Here I boil the rice until it is* **al dente,** *drain it, then toss it with peppery arugula and creamy mozzarella (try to buy mozzarella packed in water for the freshest flavor).*

4 quarts water

1½ cups Arborio rice

2 teaspoons salt, plus more to taste

6 ounces mozzarella cheese, shredded (about 1 cup)

¼ cup freshly grated Parmesan cheese

1 tablespoon unsalted butter

1 small bunch arugula, stems trimmed and coarsely chopped

1. Bring the water to a boil in a large saucepan. Add the rice and salt. Bring back to a boil and continue to boil, stirring occasionally, until the rice is tender, 15 to 17 minutes.

2. Drain the rice in a colander and put it back in the hot pot. Stir in the cheeses, butter, and arugula. Adjust the salt and serve immediately.

makes 4 servings

boiled arborio rice with lemon and parmesan

Lemon *gives this rice dish its sprightly flavor, and an egg yolk adds color and binds it together. Serve with breaded chicken or veal cutlets.*

4 quarts water

1½ cups Arborio rice

2 teaspoons salt, plus more to taste

1 large egg yolk

¼ cup freshly grated Parmesan cheese, plus more for serving

2 tablespoons fresh lemon juice

½ teaspoon grated lemon zest

2 tablespoons unsalted butter

6 fresh sage leaves, finely chopped

1. Bring the water to a boil in a large saucepan. Add the rice and salt. Bring back to a boil and continue to boil, stirring occasionally, until the rice is tender, 15 to 17 minutes.

2. Combine the egg yolk, cheese, and lemon juice and zest in a small bowl. Drain the rice in a colander and put it back in the hot pot. Stir in egg-and-lemon mixture so that it is completely combined with the rice. Cover the pot and let stand for 1 minute. Stir in the butter and sage, adjust the salt, and serve immediately with additional grated Parmesan on the side.

makes 4 servings

boiled arborio rice with smoked salmon and capers

A favorite *hors d'oeuvre, smoked salmon and capers on buttered toast, inspired this dish. Serve with a green salad for a simple but luxurious dinner.*

4 quarts water

1½ cups Arborio rice

2 teaspoons salt, plus more to taste

3 ounces thinly sliced smoked salmon, cut into ¼-inch dice

2 tablespoons unsalted butter

2 tablespoons capers, rinsed and drained

1 tablespoon finely chopped fresh parsley leaves

Freshly ground black pepper to taste

1. Bring the water to a boil in a large saucepan. Add the rice and salt. Bring back to a boil and continue to boil, stirring occasionally, until the rice is tender, 15 to 17 minutes.

2. Drain the rice in a colander and put it back in the hot pot. Stir in the salmon, butter, capers, and parsley, season with salt and pepper, and serve immediately.

makes 4 servings

polenta with three cheeses

When I want to *experience the guilty pleasure of Italian cheese, I go all the way. Buy best-quality cheese from a reputable gourmet store or Italian deli, since that's what this dish is all about.*

4 cups water

½ teaspoon salt, plus more to taste

I cup quick-cooking grits or instant polenta

⅓ cup freshly grated Parmesan cheese

⅓ cup crumbled Gorgonzola cheese

⅓ cup mascarpone

Freshly ground black pepper to taste

I. Bring the water and salt to a boil in a medium-size saucepan. Slowly stir in the grits or polenta. Reduce the heat to low and cook for 5 minutes, stirring often until the polenta is thick and smooth.

2. Stir in the cheeses and cook until everything is well combined and the cheeses are melted, I to 2 minutes. Season with salt and pepper. Spoon the polenta into four bowls and serve immediately.

makes 4 side-dish servings or
2 main-course servings

polenta with fresh corn and chives

There's something *surprising yet natural about mixing fresh corn kernels into cornmeal mush. The two ingredients have contrasting textures and complementary flavors. A handful of chopped chives and an optional sprinkling of grated Cheddar make this one of the freshest, most satisfying side dishes I know.*

4 cups water

½ teaspoon salt, plus more to taste

I cup quick-cooking grits or instant polenta

I cup fresh corn kernels (from 2 small ears)

¼ cup finely chopped fresh chives

2 tablespoons unsalted butter

½ cup grated Cheddar cheese (optional)

Freshly ground black pepper to taste

I. Bring the water and salt to a boil in a medium-size saucepan. Slowly stir in the grits or polenta. Reduce the heat to low and cook about 5 minutes, stirring often, until the polenta is thick and smooth.

2. Stir in the corn, chives, butter, and cheese if desired and cook until everything is well combined and the cheese is melted, I to 2 minutes. Season with salt and pepper. Spoon the polenta into four bowls and serve immediately.

makes 4 servings

polenta with swiss chard and simmered tomato sauce

Slightly bitter *Swiss chard is cooked right along with polenta. A simple simmered tomato sauce, enriched with cream if you like, makes this a colorful as well as delicious first course or vegetarian entree.*

One 28-ounce can crushed tomatoes

1 medium-size carrot, peeled and finely chopped

1 small onion, peeled and finely chopped

1 tablespoon extra-virgin olive oil

1 teaspoon salt, plus more to taste

¼ cup heavy cream (optional)

Freshly ground black pepper to taste

4 cups water

1 cup quick-cooking grits or instant polenta

1 large bunch Swiss chard, washed, stems removed, and leaves coarsely chopped

1. Combine the tomatoes, carrot, onion, olive oil, and ½ teaspoon of the salt in a large saucepan and bring to a simmer over medium heat. Cook, partially covered, until slightly thickened, 30 to 40 minutes. Puree in the blender or food processor, in batches if necessary, and return to the pot. Stir in the heavy cream, if desired. Season with salt and pepper.

2. Bring the water and the remaining ½ teaspoon salt to a boil in a medium-size saucepan. Slowly stir in the grits or polenta, then stir in the greens. Reduce the heat to low and cook until the

polenta is thick and smooth, about 5 minutes, stirring often. Season with salt and pepper. Spoon the polenta into four bowls, spoon some tomato sauce over each, and serve immediately.

makes 4 first-course servings or
2 main-course servings

pearl barley with sunflower seeds and dried cherries

Barley's nutty flavor *is enhanced by the addition of crunchy seeds and chewy dried fruit. Dried cherries are available at natural food stores and in many supermarkets. Serve as a side dish with roast chicken or game hens.*

2 cups homemade chicken stock (page 8) or canned low-sodium chicken broth

2¼ cups water

2 tablespoons extra-virgin olive oil

2 cups pearl barley

½ cup shelled sunflower seeds

½ cup dried cherries or currants

1 tablespoon finely chopped fresh parsley leaves

Salt and freshly ground black pepper to taste

1. Bring the chicken stock, water, and olive oil to a boil in a large saucepan. Add the barley, reduce the heat to medium-low, cover, and simmer until tender, 30 to 35 minutes.

2. Stir in the sunflower seeds, cherries, and parsley, season with salt and pepper, and serve.

makes 4 servings

pearl barley and pesto

Pesto marries very well *with earthy barley. Chicken stock flavors the barley nicely, but water may be substituted if you like.*

2 cups homemade chicken stock (page 8) or canned low-sodium chicken broth

2¼ cups water

2 cups pearl barley

2 tablespoons walnuts or pine nuts

2 cups tightly packed fresh basil leaves, washed and dried

I garlic clove, peeled

½ cup extra-virgin olive oil

¼ cup freshly grated Parmesan cheese

Salt and freshly ground black pepper to taste

I. Bring the chicken stock and water to boil in a large saucepan. Add the barley, reduce the heat to medium-low, cover, and simmer until tender, 30 to 35 minutes.

2. While the barley is cooking, make the pesto. Combine the nuts, basil, and garlic in the work bowl of a food processor or blender and process until finely chopped, scraping down the sides of the bowl two or three times as necessary. With the motor running, add the olive oil in a slow, steady stream. Scrape the mixture into a small bowl, stir in the cheese, and season with salt and pepper.

3. When the barley is cooked, stir in the pesto and serve.

makes 4 servings

pearl barley, porcini, and parmesan

I've borrowed *the flavors of a favorite risotto for this dish. Creamy and wonderfully textured, barley is just as satisfying as risotto, without any of the stirring.*

½ ounce dried porcini mushrooms

I cup boiling water

2½ cups homemade chicken stock (page 8) or canned low-sodium chicken broth

I cup dry white wine

I small onion, peeled and finely chopped

2 cups pearl barley

¾ cup freshly grated Parmesan cheese

¼ cup finely chopped fresh parsley leaves

3 tablespoons unsalted butter

Salt and freshly ground black pepper to taste

I. Place the porcini in a small heatproof bowl and cover with the boiling water. Let stand until rehydrated, about 30 minutes. Drain, reserving the liquid, and coarsely chop.

2. Strain the mushroom liquid through a fine sieve lined with cheesecloth or paper towels. Bring ¾ cup of the strained mushroom liquid, the chicken stock, wine, and onion to a boil in a large saucepan. Add the barley, reduce the heat to medium-low, cover, and simmer for I5 minutes. Stir in the mushrooms, cover, and simmer until tender, another I5 to 20 minutes.

3. Stir in the Parmesan, parsley, and butter. Season with salt and pepper and serve immediately.

makes 4 servings

bulgur with spinach and cashews

Some favorite *ingredients from Indian cooking—spinach, cashews, lime juice—give healthy and quick-cooking bulgur an infusion of flavor.*

¾ cup fine bulgur

I cup water

½ teaspoon salt, plus more to taste

6 ounces fresh spinach, washed, tough stems removed, and leaves coarsely chopped

I tablespoon extra-virgin olive oil

I tablespoon fresh lime juice

½ teaspoon curry powder

¼ cup roasted cashews, coarsely chopped

Freshly ground black pepper to taste

I. Place the bulgur in a large heatproof bowl. Bring the water and salt to a boil in a large saucepan. Stir in the spinach and cook until wilted, I to 2 minutes. Pour the spinach and water over the bulgur, stir, cover with plastic wrap, and let stand for 15 minutes.

2. Combine the olive oil, lime juice, and curry powder in a small bowl. Fluff the bulgur and spinach with a fork and stir in the dressing and cashews. Season with salt and pepper and serve warm or refrigerate up to I day and bring to room temperature before serving.

makes 4 servings

bulgur and carrots with cumin-coriander dressing

One day, *I used some leftover Tunisian carrot salad to moisten some bulgur. I loved the combination, and it has become a regular side dish when I serve grilled chicken or lamb brochettes.*

2 medium-size carrots, peeled and grated

½ medium-size red bell pepper, seeded and cut into ¼-inch dice

6 black olives, pitted and coarsely chopped

1 tablespoon orange juice

1 tablespoon fresh lemon juice

1 tablespoon extra-virgin olive oil

½ teaspoon ground coriander

½ teaspoon ground cumin

Pinch of ground cinnamon

¼ teaspoon hot red pepper flakes

¾ cup fine bulgur

1 cup water

½ teaspoon salt, plus more to taste

1. Combine the carrots, bell pepper, olives, juices, olive oil, coriander, cumin, cinnamon, and red pepper flakes in a medium-size bowl. Cover with plastic wrap and refrigerate until ready to use, up to 6 hours.

2. Place the bulgur in a large heatproof bowl. Bring the water and salt to boil in a large saucepan. Pour the water over the

bulgur, stir, cover with plastic wrap, and let stand for 15 minutes.

3. Fluff the bulgur with a fork and stir in the carrot mixture. Season with salt and

serve warm or refrigerate up to 1 day and bring to room temperature before serving.

makes 4 servings

walnut-tarragon quinoa

Super-nutritious *and pleasantly crunchy, quinoa is an interesting alternative to rice, couscous, orzo, or barley. This dish can be made several hours in advance, refrigerated, and reheated in the microwave.*

1 cup quinoa

2 cups water

½ cup walnuts, coarsely chopped

1 tablespoon chopped fresh tarragon leaves

1 teaspoon tarragon vinegar

1 tablespoon extra-virgin olive oil

Salt and freshly ground black pepper to taste

1. Rinse the quinoa under cold water in a fine strainer to remove any bitter residue. Combine the quinoa and water in a medium-size saucepan and bring to a boil. Reduce the heat to medium-low and simmer until the quinoa is tender, 15 to 20 minutes. Remove the pan from the heat and fluff the quinoa with a fork.

2. Transfer the quinoa to a large serving bowl. Stir in the remaining ingredients and serve.

makes 4 servings

quinoa with prosciutto, figs, and mint

Although quinoa *is an ancient South American grain, I like the way it combines with Mediterranean ingredients like figs and mint.*

1 cup quinoa

2 cups water

2 ounces sliced prosciutto, finely chopped

3 dried Calmyrna figs, stems removed and coarsely chopped

2 tablespoons finely chopped fresh mint leaves

2 tablespoons pine nuts

1 tablespoon extra-virgin olive oil

1 teaspoon fresh lemon juice

Salt and freshly ground black pepper to taste

1. Rinse the quinoa under cold water in a fine strainer to remove any bitter residue. Combine the quinoa and water in a medium-size saucepan and bring to a boil. Reduce the heat to medium-low and simmer until the quinoa is tender, 15 to 20 minutes. Remove the pan from the heat and fluff the quinoa with a fork.

2. Transfer the quinoa to a large serving bowl. Stir in the remaining ingredients and serve.

makes 4 servings

boiled dinners

Hearty Beef Stew

•

Boiled Beef with Salsa Verde

•

Corned Beef and Cabbage

•

Beef Short Ribs with Exotic Spices

•

Beer-Braised Short Ribs

•

Blanquette of Veal

•

Braised Pork Roast with Yams

•

Braised Pork with Chipotle Chiles

•

Asian-Style Stewed Pork with Water Chestnuts and Snow Peas

•

Red Beans, Sausages, and Rice

•

Green Lentils with Poached Sausage

•

Chinese Chicken Salad Packages

•

Chicken Breasts Poached in Wild Mushroom Broth

•

continued

Chicken and Rice

◆

Moroccan-Flavored Chicken and Couscous

◆

Cold Poached Salmon with Tomato-Mint Salsa

◆

Salmon Poached in White Wine over Warm Potato and Ham Salad

◆

Cod Fillets in Fennel Broth

◆

Spaghetti and Clams in Hearty Tomato Sauce

◆

Clams in Thai-Seasoned Broth

◆

Mussels in Belgian Beer

◆

Mussels in White Wine over Spaghetti

◆

Boiled Lobsters with Lemon-Caper Mayonnaise

◆

Plain and Simple Shrimp Boil

◆

Squid with Saffron Couscous

◆

Scallops Simmered in Spiced Tomato Broth

◆

"Sure," you say. "Pasta is one thing. But what if I want a soul-satisfying plateful of beef or a nice piece of fish? Are you telling me that I can boil up some *real* food?"

I'll admit that hearty entrees are not what first came to mind when I began to think about boiling. Boiled beef? Boiled chicken? I wasn't writing a book for hospital patients or self-denying dieters, after all. Then I remembered the garlicky corned beef and cabbage my mother used to make, adapted from a trusty James Beard cookbook. Wasn't that just a few ingredients thrown into a big pot of water? Or the luxurious veal blanquette I try to make at least once a winter—the meat isn't browned, but simply simmered with the other ingredients.

Boiling has a bad rep for leaching flavor from food. But used wisely it can actually enhance flavor and texture. In many of the recipes that follow, meat, chicken, fish, or seafood is cooked in a relatively small amount of liquid. This liquid—water, stock, wine, juice, or a combination of these—seasons the food and keeps it moist. In many cases, the liquid itself becomes an intensely flavored sauce or broth that moistens the finished dish as well as an accompaniment of crusty bread, pasta, or rice.

Tough, inexpensive cuts of meat become yielding when slowly simmered in liquid (see page 7 for more on simmering). Most recipes for stews and simmered roasts call for the browning of meat before adding liquid. The idea is that browning seals in flavor and gives the meat a caramelized crust before the liquid is added. But is browning necessary for flavor and texture if the meat is cooked in a highly seasoned liquid for such a long time?

At the suggestion of Mark Bittman, author of "The Minimalist" column in the *New York Times* food section and an expert on streamlining and simplifying recipes, I tried stewing various cuts without browning. I was very happy with the results. You can make an excellent Hearty Beef Stew by skipping this step. A highly seasoned red wine marinade more than makes up for any flavor sacrificed with the browning. Likewise, short ribs, a flavorful but extremely chewy cut of beef, become fall-off-the-bone tender when gently simmered for several hours. No need to brown them for flavor, since they have a nice long time to absorb the five-spice powder, ginger, orange, and soy sauce added to the cooking liquid.

If you crave something meaty but don't have time for a slow simmer, try the Green Lentils with Poached Sausage. The sausage

and highly seasoned dressing lend flavor to the dish without the long cooking time required of most stews.

If you can boil water, you can poach chicken breasts (see Perfect Poached Chicken Breasts, page 10). This technique has several things going for it aside from simplicity. It's a no-fat way to prepare chicken. Done correctly, it results in incredibly moist meat. And it is versatile. If you can poach chicken breasts you can make an infinite variety of chicken salads, like the hoisin-flavored example on page 185. Chicken Breasts Poached in Wild Mushroom Broth (page 189) makes a spare and elegant one-dish meal. For something heartier, poach breasts in chicken stock and then cook

vibrantly flavored couscous or creamy rice in the same liquid. I love the efficient way the stock is used twice in these recipes.

Inexpensive stew meats cook up wonderfully, but with chicken breasts, it's worth it to spend a little extra. Most mass-produced chickens are rubbery and tasteless regardless of how you cook them. It's not necessary to buy expensive free-range chicken, but do seek out quality brands like Empire or Bell and Evans. Take care not to overcook the breasts or let the water come to a full boil—otherwise, instead of juicy, tender meat you'll get shrunken, rubbery chicken that no amount of mayonnaise can redeem.

Have you ever spent $10.95 a pound or more on salmon fillets only to dry them out with a few too many minutes under the broiler? Even if you've cooked them to moist perfection, you still have to live with the smell of sizzling fish for days afterward. Poaching, on the other hand, is a neat, foolproof method for perfectly cooked fish (see Perfect Poached Salmon, page 11). There is absolutely no danger of overcooking. Place the fillets in a pot of simmering water, cover, and turn the heat off. Half an hour later lift your perfectly cooked salmon from the pot and serve with Tomato-Mint Salsa or any of the flavored mayonnaises on pages 209–210. Just a little bit more advanced is Cod Fillets in Fennel Broth. Carrots, onions, and fennel are boiled to make a poaching liquid. Additional fennel and potatoes are cooked along with the fish and make a tasty vegetable accompaniment. A bonus for the health-conscious: it's practically fat free.

Moist heat is perfect for shellfish, too. Here, it is essential to watch the pot carefully and remove it from the heat as soon as your seafood is just cooked. Clams and mussels need only a few minutes in a pot of a little boiling liquid to open up. The resulting broth is great for dipping both the seafood and moistening some pasta or lots of crusty bread. Technically, you don't even have to boil the shrimp for the Plain and Simple Shrimp Boil. Just throw them into a boiling pot of spicy broth, turn off the heat, and let sit for five minutes. This way you avoid any possibility of rubbery, overcooked shrimp. Squid and scallops also cook almost on contact with simmering liquid. Remove from the heat the very second they become opaque and you'll be rewarded with tender, briny morsels to serve either in their own cooking liquid or over a bed of fluffy rice or couscous.

hearty beef stew

This hearty *and warming stew is also remarkably easy because there's no browning. The beef is marinated in a garlicky wine mixture for great flavor, and then the whole thing is simply simmered until done. Serve with buttered egg noodles or lots of crusty bread to soak up the juices.*

8 garlic cloves, peeled and finely chopped

2½ pounds beef chuck, trimmed of fat and cut into 1-inch cubes

1 large onion, peeled and coarsely chopped

4 medium-size carrots, peeled and cut into ¼-inch-thick rounds

Salt and freshly ground black pepper to taste

1 tablespoon red wine vinegar

1 cup dry red wine

½ teaspoon dried thyme

1 bay leaf

1. Combine all the ingredients in a large bowl, cover with plastic wrap, and refriger-ate for at least an hour and up to 24 hours, stirring up the mixture several times.

2. Place the meat mixture in a large saucepan over medium-high heat. Bring to a boil, reduce the heat to medium-low, and cover. Simmer gently until the meat is tender, 1 to 1½ hours. Remove the meat with a slotted spoon and place in a bowl. Increase the heat to high and boil the liquid, uncovered, to reduce and slightly thicken it, 5 to 7 minutes. Return the meat to the pot to heat through, another 2 minutes, then serve.

makes 4 servings

boiled beef with salsa verde

Although *"boiled beef" might sound unbearably bland, this recipe, adapted from Marcella Hazan, actually makes a delicious dinner just like your mom might have made (if she was a great Italian cook). Adding the brisket to already boiling water seals in flavor in the same way that browning or frying would. Cooking in water has the added advantage of tenderizing this rather tough cut while helping to retain its moisture. I like to serve thin slices of warm or cold boiled beef with a sparkling green sauce made with bell peppers and cilantro, although horseradish or mustard make even simpler and quicker accompaniments.*

2 quarts water

1 celery stalk with leaves still attached

1 medium-size carrot, peeled

1 medium-size onion, peeled and quartered

One 4-pound center-cut brisket, trimmed of all visible fat

2 teaspoons salt, plus more to taste

1 large garlic clove, peeled

½ medium-size green bell pepper, seeded and cut into a few pieces

1 cup tightly packed fresh cilantro leaves

2 tablespoons capers, well drained

½ cup extra-virgin olive oil

2 tablespoons fresh lemon juice

1. Place the water, celery, carrot, and onion in a large pot or Dutch oven and bring to a boil. Add the brisket, cover, and return to a boil. Reduce the heat to medium-low and simmer, covered, for 1½ hours. Add the salt to the cooking

water, cover, and simmer until the meat is tender when pierced with a skewer or sharp paring knife, another 1½ to 2 hours.

2. Meanwhile, make the salsa verde. Combine the garlic, bell pepper, cilantro, and capers in the work bowl of a food processor or blender and process until smooth, scraping down the sides once or twice as necessary. With the motor running, pour the olive oil and then the lemon juice into the feed tube.

Scrape the mixture into a small bowl, season with salt, cover with plastic wrap, and set aside.

3. Transfer the meat to a cutting board, cover with aluminum foil, and let rest for 10 minutes. Cut against the grain into ¼-inch-thick slices. Serve warm (or refrigerate before slicing, slice later, and serve cold) with the salsa verde on the side.

makes 6 servings

corned beef and cabbage

Corned beef and cabbage *was a favorite in my house when I was growing up. We loved it as a change from the stronger, saltier corned beef from the local kosher deli. Trim all visible fat from the corned beef so you have a flavorful but not greasy broth in which to cook the vegetables. Cook the vegetables until just tender. Serve with mustard, horseradish, and fresh rye bread on the side.*

1 corned beef brisket, about 6 pounds

4 garlic cloves, peeled and thinly sliced

1 large yellow onion, peeled

2 whole cloves

1 teaspoon fennel seeds

24 baby carrots, or 8 large carrots, peeled, cut in half, and thin ends halved, thick ends quartered

1½ pounds small (golf ball size) white or red potatoes

¾ pound small (golf ball size) boiling onions, peeled

1 small cabbage, sliced in half down the center, then cut into 1-inch-thick wedges

1. Trim the corned beef of visible fat, rinse thoroughly under cold water, and pat dry. Cut small slits in the corned beef with a sharp paring knife and place a sliver of garlic in each slit. Place the corned beef in a large pot or Dutch oven. Cover by 1 inch with cold water and bring to a boil. Boil for 5 to 7 minutes, skimming off the gray foam that

forms on the surface with a large spoon. Stick the yellow onion with the cloves and add it to the pot along with the fennel seeds. Reduce the heat to medium-low, cover, and simmer until the meat feels tender when the thickest part is pierced with a skewer, 2 to 3 hours.

2. Transfer the meat to a cutting board and cover with aluminum foil to keep warm. Remove and discard the yellow onion. Increase the heat to high under the pot, add the carrots, potatoes, and boiling onions, and bring to a boil. Reduce the heat to medium-low, cover, and simmer for 10 minutes. Add the cabbage and cook until all the vegetables are tender, another 10 to 15 minutes.

3. Drain the vegetables. Slice the corned beef against the grain into ¼-inch-thick slices. Arrange the meat on a platter and surround with the carrots, potatoes, onions, and cabbage. Serve immediately.

makes 6 to 8 servings

beef short ribs
with exotic spices

When you want *something stick-to-your-ribs but also a little unusual, try this simple recipe over Perfect White Rice (page 6). Five-spice powder (look for it in the Asian section of the supermarket) is a blend of star anise, cloves, cinnamon, fennel seed, and pepper. Along with some ground ginger, it is a quick and interesting way to flavor hearty beef short ribs. Cook this dish a day ahead, if you can. Its flavors improve in the refrigerator overnight, and before reheating it you can easily remove the fat that's risen to the top of the pot.*

2 quarts water

¼ cup soy sauce

1 cup Scotch whiskey

6 scallions, white and light green parts, finely chopped

¼ cup packed chopped fresh cilantro leaves

2 tablespoons sugar

2 tablespoons five-spice powder

2 teaspoons ground ginger

Zest from 1 orange, removed with a vegetable peeler

4 pounds beef short ribs

Salt to taste

1. Combine the water, soy sauce, Scotch, scallions, cilantro, sugar, five-spice powder, ginger, and zest in a Dutch oven and

bring to a boil. Reduce the heat to medium-low and simmer for 10 minutes to blend the flavors. Add the short ribs and simmer, partially covered, until the meat is tender and almost falling off the bone, about 2 hours.

2. Remove the ribs from the pot with a slotted spoon and set aside. Remove the zest and discard. Increase the heat to high and reduce the liquid, stirring frequently, until it thickens slightly, about 15 minutes. Season the sauce with salt, if necessary. Return the ribs to the pot and simmer until heated through, 2 to 3 minutes, then serve.

makes 4 servings

beer-braised short ribs

Use the darkest beer *possible here. Not only will dark beer contribute to the dish's rich flavor, it will give the sauce a rich color, important when you are not going to brown the meat.*

Two 12-ounce bottles dark beer

6½ cups water

1 medium-size onion, peeled and finely chopped

2 garlic cloves, peeled and finely chopped

2 tablespoons firmly packed brown sugar

1 tablespoon cider vinegar

1 teaspoon salt

1 bay leaf

1 teaspoon dried thyme

4 pounds beef short ribs

1 tablespoon Dijon mustard

¼ cup finely chopped fresh parsley leaves

1. Combine the beer, water, onion, garlic, sugar, vinegar, salt, bay leaf, and thyme in a large saucepan or Dutch oven and bring to a boil. Reduce the heat to a simmer and cook for 10 minutes to blend the flavors. Add the short ribs and simmer, partially covered, until the meat is tender and almost falling off the bone, about 2 hours.

2. Remove the ribs from the pot with a slotted spoon and set aside. Remove the bay leaf and discard. Increase the heat to high and reduce the liquid, stirring frequently, until it thickens slightly, about 15 minutes. Skim the fat from the surface of the sauce and discard. Stir in the mus-

tard and parsley and season the sauce with salt if necessary. Add the ribs back to the pot and simmer until heated through, 2 to 3 minutes.

makes 6 servings

blanquette of veal

A blanquette *is traditionally cooked without browning, making it a natural for* Just Add Water. *Egg yolks and heavy cream enrich the sauce and thicken it. The yolks need to be "tempered" so they won't curdle and resemble scrambled eggs when added to the hot blanquette. Do this by slowly pouring a little of the hot cooking liquid into the eggs before stirring them into the blanquette. Serve over wide egg noodles.*

2½ pounds boneless veal shoulder, trimmed of fat and cut into 1½-inch cubes

1½ cups dry white wine

1½ cups homemade chicken stock (page 8) or canned low-sodium chicken broth

1 medium-size onion, peeled

2 garlic cloves, peeled and crushed

1 bay leaf

½ teaspoon salt, plus more to taste

Freshly ground black pepper to taste

¼ teaspoon dried thyme

¼ teaspoon ground nutmeg

10 ounces mushrooms, cleaned and thinly sliced

½ cup heavy cream

2 large egg yolks

2 tablespoons fresh lemon juice

1. Combine the veal, wine, chicken stock, onion, garlic, bay leaf, ½ teaspoon salt, pepper, thyme, and nutmeg in a large pot or Dutch oven and bring to a boil. Reduce the heat to medium-low, cover, and simmer until the meat is fork tender, about 1½ hours.

2. Remove the meat from the pot with a slotted spoon. Bring the cooking liquid to a boil and reduce to about 1½ cups, 5 to 7 minutes (you can do this by eye, or you can pour it into a heatproof glass measuring cup periodically to see how it's doing). Add the mushrooms, heavy cream, and meat to the pot and bring back to a boil. Reduce the heat to medium-low and simmer for 5 minutes.

3. Whisk together the egg yolks and lemon juice in a small bowl. Continue to whisk and slowly dribble in ¼ cup of the hot cooking liquid. Stir the egg mixture into the blanquette and simmer until the liquid begins to thicken, 2 to 3 minutes. Season with salt and pepper. Remove from heat and cover to keep warm until serving.

makes 4 servings

braised pork roast with yams

Yams, *cumin, and a little bit of oregano give this roast a South American flavor.*
Serve with Lentils in Habanero Oil (page 95) and Perfect White Rice (page 6).

1 boneless pork roast, 2½ to 3 pounds

4 garlic cloves, peeled and thinly sliced

Salt and freshly ground black pepper to taste

2 cups water

¼ cup soy sauce

2 tablespoons red wine vinegar

2 tablespoons firmly packed brown sugar

2 teaspoons ground cumin

4 yams (about 2 pounds), peeled and cut into 1-inch-thick slices

2 medium-size onions, peeled and quartered

2 tablespoons chopped fresh oregano leaves

Salt and freshly ground black pepper to taste

1. Cut small slits in the pork roast with a sharp paring knife and place a silver of garlic in each slit. Sprinkle the pork roast generously with salt and pepper. Combine the pork, water, soy sauce, vinegar, brown sugar, and cumin in a large pot or Dutch oven. Bring to a boil, reduce the heat to medium-low, and simmer, covered, turning the pork occasionally, until fork tender, 1½ to 2 hours.

2. Transfer the roast to a carving board and cover with aluminum foil to keep warm. Add the yams and onions to the cooking liquid and bring back to a boil. Reduce the heat to medium-low and simmer until the vegetables are soft, about 15 minutes. Stir in the oregano and season with salt and pepper.

3. Carve the roast into ½-inch-thick slices. Place several slices on each of four dinner plates and top with some of the vegetables and juices.

makes 4 servings

braised pork with chipotle chiles

Chipotle chiles, *available in Latin markets and many supermarkets, give this easy stew so much flavor that you really won't miss browning the meat before braising. Serve over Perfect White Rice (page 6) or Polenta with Fresh Corn and Chives (page 147).*

2 pounds boneless pork shoulder or pork rib end, trimmed of fat and cut into 2-inch chunks

½ cup red wine vinegar

1½ cups homemade chicken stock (page 8) or canned low-sodium chicken broth

3 canned chipotle chiles in adobo, finely chopped

3 tablespoons adobo sauce from the can

8 garlic cloves, peeled and crushed

¼ cup packed chopped fresh cilantro leaves

Salt to taste

1. Combine the pork, vinegar, chicken stock, chipotles, adobo sauce, and garlic in a large pot or Dutch oven. Bring to a boil, reduce the heat to medium-low, and simmer, covered, stirring occasionally, until the pork is tender, about 1 hour and 15 minutes.

2. Remove the pork from the pot with a slotted spoon. Boil the liquid to reduce and slightly thicken it, 5 to 7 minutes. Stir in the pork and cilantro, season with salt, and simmer until heated through, 2 to 3 minutes.

makes 4 servings

asian-style stewed pork with water chestnuts and snow peas

This dish *has all the lively flavors of a stir-fry, but with the rich cooking juices that only come from a stew. Serve with Perfect White Rice (page 6) or Asian-style egg noodles.*

2 pounds boneless pork shoulder or pork rib end, trimmed of fat and cut into 2-inch chunks

1 cup homemade chicken stock (page 8) or canned low-sodium chicken broth

½ cup rice wine vinegar

¼ cup soy sauce

2 tablespoons Asian sesame oil

One 1-inch piece fresh gingerroot, peeled and thinly sliced

8 garlic cloves, peeled and crushed

One 8-ounce can water chestnuts, rinsed, drained, and thinly sliced

¼ pound snow peas, washed and strings removed

4 scallions, white and light green parts, finely chopped

Salt to taste

1. Combine the pork, chicken stock, vinegar, soy sauce, sesame oil, ginger, and garlic in a large pot or Dutch oven. Bring to a boil, reduce the heat to medium-low, and simmer, covered, stirring occasionally, until the pork is tender, about 1 hour and 15 minutes.

continued

2. Remove the pork from the pot with a slotted spoon. Boil the liquid to reduce and slightly thicken it, 5 to 7 minutes. Stir in the pork, water chestnuts, snow peas, and scallions, season with salt, and simmer over medium heat until the snow peas are tender, 3 to 4 minutes.

makes 4 servings

red beans, sausages, and rice

In this recipe, *two pots, rather than one, are brought to a boil—the beans and rice are cooked separately and stirred together at the end. But don't let this minor complication deter you. When you want a simple, comforting meal that's also well seasoned with some unusual flavors, give this a try.*

2 cups dried red or kidney beans, rinsed and picked over for stones

6½ cups water

½ pound kielbasa or other smoked sausage, cut into ¼-inch-thick rounds

1 large onion, peeled and finely chopped

2 garlic cloves, peeled and finely chopped

1 small fennel bulb, trimmed and finely chopped

2 bay leaves

1 teaspoon sweet paprika

¼ teaspoon dried thyme

¼ teaspoon cayenne pepper

1 tablespoon fresh lemon juice

Salt and freshly ground black pepper to taste

1 cup long-grain white rice

¼ cup finely chopped fresh parsley leaves

6 scallions, white and light green parts, finely chopped

1. Combine the beans, 5 cups of the water, the kielbasa, onion, garlic, fennel, bay leaves, paprika, thyme, and cayenne in a large pot or Dutch oven. Bring to a boil, reduce the heat to medium-low, and simmer, partially covered, until the beans are tender and most of the liquid

has been absorbed, I to I½ hours. Stir in the lemon juice and season with salt and black pepper.

2. While the beans are cooking, combine the rice, the remaining I½ cups water, the parsley, and ½ teaspoon salt. Bring to a boil, cover, turn the heat to low, and cook until the liquid has been absorbed and the rice is tender, I2 to I5 minutes.

3. Spoon the beans and the rice into a large bowl. Stir to combine. Sprinkle the scallions over the top before serving.

makes 6 to 8 servings

green lentils with poached sausage

This is a *completely satisfying and wholesome meal, with a touch of sophistication because of its French origins. The lentils, potatoes, and sausage must be boiled separately, but that's as difficult as it gets. Green lentils, valued for their flavor and the way they keep their shape during cooking, are available at gourmet shops, natural food stores, and many supermarkets. French garlic sausage is traditional, but I also like Italian sausage with lots of fennel flavor.*

I cup green or brown lentils, rinsed and picked over for stones

I medium-size onion, peeled

I medium-size carrot, peeled

2 garlic cloves, peeled

1½ quarts water

¼ cup extra-virgin olive oil

I pound French garlic sausage or sweet Italian sausage

1½ pounds small red potatoes

¼ cup white wine vinegar

I tablespoon Dijon mustard

I medium-size shallot, finely chopped

2 tablespoons finely chopped fresh parsley leaves

I tablespoon finely chopped fresh tarragon leaves

Salt and freshly ground black pepper to taste

continued

1. Combine the lentils, onion, carrot, garlic, and water in a large saucepan. Bring to a boil, cover, reduce the heat to medium-low, and cook until the lentils are tender, 15 to 20 minutes. Drain the lentils and discard the onion, carrot, and garlic. Place in a large bowl, and toss with 1 tablespoon of the olive oil.

2. While the lentils are cooking, boil the sausage. Prick the sausage in several places with a fork. In a medium-size saucepan, cover the sausage with water, bring to a boil, and boil until tender, 15 to 20 minutes. Drain and cut into ½-inch-thick rounds. Add to the bowl with the lentils.

3. While the lentils and sausage are cooking, cook the potatoes. In another medium-size saucepan, cover the potatoes with water, bring to a boil, and boil until tender when pierced with a knife, 20 to 25 minutes. Drain the potatoes and halve or quarter them, depending on size. Add them to the bowl with the lentils and sausage and sprinkle with 1 tablespoon of the vinegar.

4. Whisk together the remaining 3 tablespoons vinegar, the remaining 3 tablespoons olive oil, the mustard, shallot, parsley, and tarragon in a small bowl. Toss the dressing with the lentils, sausage, and potatoes. Season with salt and pepper and serve warm or refrigerate up to 6 hours and bring to room temperature before serving.

makes 4 servings

chinese chicken salad packages

Poached chicken breasts *are the basis of this flavorful salad, which is wrapped in lettuce leaves for easy, healthy eating. (Instead of wrapping, you can simply serve the chicken over the lettuce if you like.) Jicama is a mild, crunchy root vegetable similar in taste and texture to water chestnuts. This is a great lunch or light supper dish. Serve with Sesame Rice Salad with Asparagus (page 141).*

2 cups water

1½ teaspoons salt

2 whole boneless, skinless chicken breasts, cut into halves

¼ cup rice wine vinegar

1½ tablespoons soy sauce

3 tablespoons hoisin sauce

1 tablespoon peeled and minced fresh gingerroot

1 tablespoon Asian sesame oil

2 tablespoons vegetable oil

1 cup peeled and diced jicama

2 medium-size scallions, white and green parts, minced

2 tablespoons minced fresh cilantro leaves

8 large Boston or green lettuce leaves

1. In a large skillet, bring the water and salt to a boil. Reduce the heat to a simmer and add the chicken breasts. Cover and cook at a bare simmer for 5 minutes. Turn the chicken, cover, and cook for another 5 minutes. Remove the skillet from the heat, uncover, and let the chicken stand in the poaching liquid for 30 minutes. *continued*

2. Whisk the vinegar, soy sauce, hoisin sauce, ginger, sesame oil, and vegetable oil together in a small bowl.

3. Remove the chicken from the poaching liquid and shred by hand into bite-size pieces. Combine the chicken, jicama, scallions, and cilantro in a large bowl. Toss with the dressing. Spoon several tablespoons of the salad onto the middle of each lettuce leaf. Working one package at a time, fold the bottom quarter of each leaf up toward the middle and then form each package into a burrito shape by rolling the lettuce leaf from left to right to enclose the salad. Place two packages, seam side down, on each of four dinner plates and serve immediately.

makes 4 servings

chicken salad

Once you know how to poach chicken breasts (see page 10), making an amazing variety of chicken salads is just a matter of chopping and stirring. Dress your salad with either mayonnaise or oil and vinegar and add whatever vegetables, herbs, and spices you like. Here are some favorite combinations.

Classic American Chicken Salad: Combine 2 whole poached, shredded chicken breasts, ¾ cup mayonnaise, 1 tablespoon fresh lemon juice, 2 finely chopped celery stalks, 2 tablespoons finely chopped fresh parsley leaves, and salt and pepper to taste.

Chicken, Bacon, and Avocado Salad: Omit the celery and add 1 peeled, pitted, and diced avocado and 4 strips crisp-cooked, crumbled bacon to Classic American Chicken Salad.

Curried Chicken Salad with Mango: Add 1 peeled, pitted, and diced mango, 1 small, finely chopped red onion, and 1 teaspoon curry powder to Classic American Chicken Salad.

Mediterranean Chicken Salad: Combine 2 whole poached, shredded chicken breasts, ¼ cup extra-virgin olive oil, 3 tablespoons red wine vinegar, 6 coarsely chopped oil-packed sun-dried tomatoes,

1 tablespoon chopped capers, 2 tablespoons chopped fresh basil leaves, and salt and pepper to taste.

Chicken Salad with Chipotle Vinaigrette: Combine 2 whole poached, shredded chicken breasts, ¼ cup extra-virgin olive oil, ¼ cup fresh lime juice, 1 finely chopped canned chipotle chile in adobo, 1 small peeled, pitted, and diced avocado, 12 halved cherry tomatoes, 2 tablespoons chopped fresh oregano leaves, and salt and pepper to taste.

Chicken Salad with Grapefruit and Ginger Vinaigrette: Combine 2 whole poached, shredded chicken breasts, 1 peeled, sectioned, and coarsely chopped red grapefruit, ¼ cup extra-virgin olive oil, 1 tablespoon Dijon mustard, 2 teaspoons grated lemon zest, 2 tablespoons fresh lemon juice, 1 tablespoon peeled and finely chopped fresh gingerroot, 2 tablespoons finely chopped fresh cilantro leaves, and salt and pepper to taste.

Chicken and Orange Salad with Sherry Vinaigrette: Combine 2 whole poached, shredded chicken breasts, ¼ cup extra-virgin olive oil, 2 tablespoons sherry wine vinegar, 2 peeled and coarsely chopped navel oranges, 2 tablespoons chopped red onion, ¼ cup pitted black olives, 2 tablespoons finely chopped fresh parsley leaves, and salt and pepper to taste.

chicken breasts poached in wild mushroom broth

If you've *taken the time to make and freeze Chicken Stock (page 8), here's one of the payoffs—a simple, comforting, low-fat chicken dish with an added flavor bonus of wild mushrooms.*

½ ounce dried wild mushrooms such as porcini

2 cups boiling water

3 cups homemade chicken stock or canned low-sodium chicken broth

24 baby carrots

12 scallions, white and light green parts, cut into 2-inch lengths

½ pound fresh shiitake mushrooms, stems removed

2 whole boneless, skinless chicken breasts, cut into halves

Salt and freshly ground black pepper to taste

1 tablespoon finely chopped fresh parsley leaves

1. Place the dried mushrooms in a small heatproof bowl and cover with the boiling water. Let stand until softened, about 15 minutes. Strain the liquid through a fine sieve lined with cheesecloth or paper towels and into a measuring cup. Reserve 1 cup. Rinse and coarsely chop the mushrooms and set aside.

2. Bring the chicken stock and the mushroom liquid to a boil in a large saucepan. Add the carrots, reduce the heat to

medium-low, and simmer for 5 minutes. Add the scallions, shiitakes, and porcini and simmer another 5 minutes. Remove the vegetables from the pan with a slotted spoon and set aside.

3. Add the chicken breasts to the barely simmering broth, cover, and cook at a bare simmer for 5 minutes. Turn the breast halves, cover, and simmer until just cooked, about 5 minutes. Transfer the chicken to a plate and cover with alu-minum foil to keep warm. Return the vegetables to the broth to heat through. Season with salt and pepper.

4. Thinly slice each chicken breast half diagonally. Place one sliced chicken breast half in each of four shallow soup plates. Ladle some broth and vegetables over each serving. Sprinkle some of the parsley on top and serve.

makes 4 servings

chicken and rice

This is a *soothing dish of white meat chicken over buttery rice, especially easy to make since the chicken gives flavor to the poaching liquid, which is then used to cook the rice. Serve with a green vegetable like Broccoli Rabe with Garlic-Chile Oil (page 48).*

2 cups homemade chicken stock
  (page 8) or canned low-sodium chicken
  broth

¾ cup dry white wine

I garlic clove, peeled and crushed

1½ teaspoons salt

2 whole boneless, skinless chicken breasts,
  cut into halves

1½ cups long-grain white rice

2 tablespoons unsalted butter

I small onion, peeled and finely chopped

2 ripe plum tomatoes, seeded and cut into
  ¼-inch dice

¼ cup finely chopped fresh parsley leaves

Freshly ground black pepper to taste

I. In a large saucepan, bring the chicken stock, wine, garlic, and salt to a boil. Reduce the heat to a simmer and add the chicken breasts. Cover and cook at a bare simmer for 5 minutes. Turn the chicken, cover, and simmer until just cooked through, another 5 minutes. Remove from the heat, uncover, and let the chicken stand in the poaching liquid for 30 minutes.

continued

2. Remove the chicken from the poaching liquid and set aside. Bring the liquid back to a boil and stir in the rice, butter, onion, and tomatoes. Reduce the heat to medium-low, cover, and simmer until tender, 15 to 20 minutes. Shred the chicken into bite-size pieces. Stir the chicken and parsley into the rice, season with salt and pepper, heat through, and serve.

makes 4 servings

moroccan-flavored chicken and couscous

A variation on *Chicken and Rice, this recipe uses spicy couscous dotted with peppers, scallions, and olives as a background for poached chicken breasts.*

2 cups homemade chicken stock (page 8) or canned low-sodium chicken broth

½ cup dry white wine

1 garlic clove, peeled and crushed

1½ teaspoons salt, plus more to taste

2 whole boneless, skinless chicken breasts, cut into halves

One 10-ounce box instant couscous

2 tablespoons extra-virgin olive oil

1 teaspoon grated lemon zest

1 teaspoon ground cumin

1 teaspoon sweet paprika

¼ teaspoon cayenne pepper

¼ cup chopped fresh parsley leaves

1 medium-size red bell pepper, seeded and cut into ¼-inch dice

2 scallions, white and green parts, finely chopped

20 Moroccan, niçoise, or other small black olives, pitted and coarsely chopped

Freshly ground black pepper to taste

1. In a large saucepan, bring the chicken stock, wine, garlic, and salt to a boil. Reduce the heat to a simmer and add the chicken breasts. Cover and cook at a bare simmer for 5 minutes. Turn the chicken, cover, and simmer until just cooked

through, another 5 minutes. Remove the from the heat, uncover, and let the chicken stand in the poaching liquid until cooked through, about 30 minutes.

2. Remove the chicken from the poaching liquid and set aside. Bring the liquid back to a boil and stir in the couscous, olive oil, lemon zest, cumin, paprika, and cayenne. Cover, remove from the heat, and let stand for 5 minutes. Fluff the couscous with a fork. Stir in the parsley, bell pepper, scallions, and olives and season with salt and pepper.

3. Divide the couscous among four dinner plates. Thinly slice each chicken breast half diagonally and place on top of the couscous. Serve immediately.

makes 4 servings

cold poached salmon with tomato-mint salsa

Poaching is *about as perfect a cooking method as you can get. It's nonfat. Your salmon won't dry out the way it can when you grill or broil. There are no strong cooking odors. Best of all, there's absolutely no way you can make an error of judgment about cooking temperature or duration, since you turn the heat off as soon as you put the fish in water and remove it exactly 30 minutes later. An extra-wide spatula is helpful in removing the fillets from the pan with no breakage. Cold poached salmon is also great with Lemon-Caper Mayonnaise (page 211).*

4 salmon fillets, about 6 ounces each

1 large ripe tomato, seeded and cut into ¼-inch dice

¼ cup chopped fresh mint leaves

1 small garlic clove, peeled and finely chopped

1 tablespoon extra-virgin olive oil

⅓ cup plain low-fat yogurt

Salt and freshly ground black pepper to taste

1 lemon, cut into 8 wedges

1. Fill a large saucepan with enough water to cover the fillets. Bring the water to a boil. With a wide spatula, carefully place the fish in the pan, cover, and turn off the heat. Let the fish sit in the water for 30 minutes. Carefully remove from the

water, again with the wide spatula. Transfer to a serving platter and refrigerate until chilled, 1 to 2 hours.

2. Combine the tomato, mint, garlic, and olive oil in a medium-size bowl. Cover and let stand at room temperature for half an hour to blend the flavors.

3. Just before you are ready to serve the salmon, combine the tomato mixture and the yogurt, then season with salt and pepper. Spoon the salsa over the fillets and serve with lemon wedges around the platter as garnish.

makes 4 servings

salmon poached in white wine over warm potato and ham salad

Broth made from *aromatic vegetables and white wine gives poached salmon a more complex flavor. Here, the fish is accompanied by a warm potato salad flecked with salty ham and dressed with white wine vinegar. In warm weather, or for the sake of convenience, both the salmon and the potato salad can be made ahead of time, refrigerated, and served cold or at room temperature.*

I medium-size onion, peeled and cut in half

I medium-size carrot, peeled and cut into 4 pieces

I celery stalk, cut into 4 pieces

3 cups dry white wine

I cup water

I tablespoon fennel seeds

8 black peppercorns

4 salmon fillets, about 6 ounces each

I½ pounds red potatoes, rinsed and scrubbed

I½ teaspoons salt

6 tablespoons extra-virgin olive oil

¼ cup white wine vinegar

I tablespoon Dijon mustard

I shallot, finely chopped

2 teaspoons capers, rinsed and drained

2 ounces sliced ham, finely chopped

3 tablespoons finely chopped fresh basil leaves

Freshly ground black pepper to taste

continued

1. Combine the onion, carrot, celery, wine, water, fennel seeds, and peppercorns in a medium-size saucepan. Bring to a boil, cover, reduce the heat to medium-low, and simmer for 20 minutes. Strain the liquid into a large saucepan and discard the solids.

2. While the broth is simmering, cook the potatoes. Place the potatoes in a large pot, cover with water, add 1 teaspoon of the salt, and bring to a boil. Continue to boil until tender (you should easily be able to insert a paring knife into a potato), 20 to 30 minutes, depending on the size of the potatoes.

3. Bring the poaching liquid to a boil. With a wide spatula, carefully place the fish in the pan, cover, and turn off the heat. Let the fish sit in the liquid for 30 minutes. Carefully remove from the liq-

uid, again with the wide spatula, and transfer to a plate. Cover the fillets with aluminum foil to keep warm or refrigerate up to 6 hours until ready to serve.

4. While the fish is poaching, finish the salad. Combine the olive oil, vinegar, mustard, shallot, capers, ham, basil, the remaining ½ teaspoon salt, and the pepper in a small bowl. Slice the warm potatoes into ¼-inch-thick rounds. Place them in a large bowl, pour all but ¼ cup of the dressing over them, and gently mix to combine. Divide the warm potato salad among four dinner plates or refrigerate up to 6 hours until ready to serve. Place a salmon fillet on top of each portion of potatoes. Drizzle the remaining dressing over the fish and serve immediately.

makes 4 servings

cod fillets in fennel broth

This is a *wonderful way to cook meaty cod fillets. The fennel and potatoes flavor the fish and make a tasty vegetable accompaniment. It's practically fat free, to boot. I like to serve this dish with thick slices of toasted country bread rubbed with a little bit of garlic, the better to soak up the broth.*

2 carrots, peeled and cut into 2-inch pieces

2 medium-size onions, peeled and quartered

1 fennel bulb, both ends trimmed and thinly sliced

6 sprigs fresh thyme

1 teaspoon fennel seeds

1 bay leaf

1 teaspoon salt, plus more to taste

½ cup dry white wine

4 cups water

¾ pound small red potatoes, sliced ¼ inch thick

Four 1-inch-thick cod fillets (about ½ pound each)

Boiling water as needed

Freshly ground black pepper to taste

1. Combine the carrots, onions, half the fennel, the thyme, fennel seeds, bay leaf, salt, wine, and water in a large sauté pan and bring to a boil. Reduce the heat to medium-low and simmer, covered, for 30 minutes. Strain the broth through a fine sieve into a large bowl. Wash the sauté pan and return the broth to the clean pan.

2. Bring the broth back to a boil, reduce

the heat to medium-low, and simmer for 5 minutes. Add the potato slices and the remaining fennel to the broth and simmer for another 5 minutes. Add the cod. If the broth does not cover the fish, add boiling water just until it does. Reduce the heat to low, cover, and cook just until the fillets are opaque, 8 to 10 minutes.

3. Carefully lift the fillets out of the pan with a large spatula and place in four shallow soup bowls. Divide the vegetables among the bowls. Season the broth with salt and pepper, pour it over the fish and vegetables, and serve.

makes 4 servings

spaghetti and clams in hearty tomato sauce

Here salty ham *provides surprising seasoning to briny clams. A little bit of tomato makes a red clam sauce for pasta. Before cooking, rinse the clams several times in several changes of cold water to ensure a grit-free sauce.*

1 cup canned crushed tomatoes

1 cup dry white wine

2 garlic cloves, peeled and crushed

1 sprig fresh rosemary

2 ounces ham, cut in 1 thick slice and cut into ¼-inch dice

1 pound spaghetti

2 tablespoons extra-virgin olive oil

4 pounds littleneck clams, rinsed several times and drained (discard any clams that won't close or have broken shells)

¼ cup chopped fresh parsley leaves

Salt and freshly ground black pepper to taste

1. Combine the tomatoes, wine, garlic, and rosemary in a large pot. Bring to a boil, reduce the heat to medium-low, and simmer until the alcohol has cooked off and the sauce has thickened, about 15 minutes. Stir in the ham and cook another 3 minutes. Remove the rosemary and garlic and discard.

2. While the sauce is cooking, bring a large pot of salted water to boil and cook the spaghetti until *al dente*, 10 to 12 minutes. Drain and toss with the olive oil.

3. Add the clams to the sauce and bring to a boil. Cover, reduce the heat to

medium-low, and simmer until the clam shells open, about 5 minutes. Discard any clams that do not open.

4. Divide the spaghetti among six serving bowls. With a slotted spoon, transfer the clams to the bowls. Stir in the parsley, season the sauce with salt if necessary, and pepper, and pour some sauce over each bowl. Serve immediately.

makes 6 servings

clams in thai-seasoned broth

Serve these clams *and their Thai-seasoned broth over rice or rice noodles. Fish sauce and rice wine are available in the Asian foods section of many supermarkets. If you can't find fresh lemongrass at your market, substitute bottled Thai Kitchen lemongrass, also available in the Asian foods section.*

2 cups rice wine

1 tablespoon Thai fish sauce (nam pla)

¼ cup fresh lime juice

¼ cup chopped fresh cilantro leaves

2 tablespoons chopped fresh mint leaves

2 tablespoons chopped fresh basil leaves

3 stalks lemongrass, trimmed and coarsely chopped, or ¼ cup finely chopped bottled lemongrass

2 shallots, peeled and coarsely chopped

8 garlic cloves, peeled and coarsely chopped

1 tablespoon peeled and coarsely chopped fresh gingerroot

½ teaspoon hot red pepper flakes

4 pounds littleneck clams, rinsed several times and drained (discard any clams that won't close or have broken shells)

Salt to taste

1. Combine the rice wine, fish sauce, lime juice, 2 tablespoons of the cilantro, the mint, basil, lemongrass, shallots, garlic, ginger, and red pepper flakes in a small saucepan. Bring to a boil, cover, reduce the heat to medium-low, and simmer for 30 minutes. Strain the broth into a large pot.

continued

2. Add the clams to the broth and bring to a boil. Cover, reduce the heat to medium-low, and simmer until the clam shells open, about 5 minutes. Discard any clams that don't open.

3. With a slotted spoon, transfer the clams to six shallow soup bowls. Season the broth with salt if necessary, and pour some broth over each bowl. Sprinkle with the remaining 2 tablespoons cilantro. Serve immediately.

makes 6 servings

mussels in belgian beer

Mussels steamed *in beer are a Belgian favorite, and it's not hard to see why. The dish couldn't be simpler to prepare, and the slightly sour beer complements the briny flavor of the mussels. If you can find Belgian beer, by all means use it, but any full-bodied beer will produce tasty mussels. Now that mussels are primarily farm-raised, there's usually no need to scrub or debeard them. Simply put them in a colander and rinse under cold water to remove any grit and dirt from the shells.*

2 shallots, peeled and finely chopped

3 garlic cloves, peeled and finely chopped

¼ cup finely chopped fresh parsley
leaves

One 12-ounce bottle Belgian or other
full-bodied beer

2 tablespoons extra-virgin olive oil

6 pounds mussels, debearded if necessary, rinsed, and drained (discard any that won't close or have broken shells)

Salt and freshly ground black pepper
to taste

I. Combine the shallots, garlic, parsley, beer, and olive oil in a large pot and bring to a boil; boil for 3 minutes to blend the flavors. Add the mussels, cover, and steam over medium-high heat until the mussel shells open, about 5 minutes. Discard any that do not open.

2. With a slotted spoon, transfer the mussels to four shallow soup bowls. Season the broth with salt and pepper and pour some broth over each bowl. Serve immediately.

makes 4 servings

mussels in white wine over spaghetti

The only thing *tricky about this dish is the timing. You want the spaghetti to be ready when the mussels are done, but you don't want to cook it too soon or it will get cold. Put the pasta in boiling water, and begin to cook the mussels 4 to 5 minutes before you think the pasta is ready. You should just have time to drain the pasta and toss it with butter when your mussels are done.*

1 tablespoon salt, plus more to taste

1 pound spaghetti

2 tablespoons unsalted butter

1 cup dry white wine

2 tablespoons chopped fresh parsley leaves

2 tablespoons chopped fresh thyme leaves

1 tablespoon chopped fresh rosemary leaves

2 garlic cloves, peeled and finely chopped

3 pounds mussels, debearded if necessary, rinsed, and drained (discard any that won't close or have broken shells)

1. Bring a large pot of water to a boil. Add the salt and spaghetti and cook until tender. Drain and toss with the butter.

2. While the spaghetti is cooking, combine the wine, parsley, thyme, rosemary, garlic, salt to taste, and mussels in a large pot and bring to a boil. Cover and steam

over medium-high heat until the mussel shells open, about 5 minutes.

3. Divide the buttered spaghetti among six serving bowls. With a slotted spoon, transfer the mussels to the bowls. Season the broth with salt if necessary, and pour some broth over each bowl. Serve immediately.

makes 6 servings

flavored mayonnaise

Homemade mayonnaise can be flavored in many different ways to complement boiled lobster, poached salmon, boiled shrimp, and steamed mussels and clams. Instead of stirring in capers and thyme, as in the recipe on page 211, try any of the following. Each recipe makes about 1 cup.

Basic Mayonnaise: Combine 1 large egg, 2 tablespoons fresh lemon juice, salt, and pepper in the work bowl of a food processor. Pulse several times to break up the egg. With the motor running, add 1 cup neutral-tasting vegetable oil such as canola oil in a steady stream and process until the mayonnaise is thick, about 1 minute. Scrape into a small bowl. Season with additional salt and pepper to taste. Refrigerate until serving.

Garlic Mayonnaise: Add 4 peeled and coarsely chopped garlic cloves to the egg, juice, salt, and pepper in the food processor. Proceed as above.

Mustard Mayonnaise: Prepare Basic Mayonnaise and stir in 1 tablespoon Dijon mustard.

Saffron Mayonnaise: Add ½ teaspoon saffron threads to the egg, juice, salt, and pepper in the food processor. Proceed as above.

Curry Mayonnaise: Prepare Basic Mayonnaise and stir in 1 tablespoon curry powder.

Basil Mayonnaise: Add ¼ cup tightly packed fresh basil leaves to the egg, juice, salt, and pepper in the food processor. Proceed as above.

Red Pepper–Garlic Mayonnaise: Add 1 bottled pimiento and 1 coarsely chopped garlic clove to the egg, juice, salt, and pepper in the food processor. Proceed as above.

Chipotle Mayonnaise: Add 2 coarsely chopped canned chipotle chiles in adobo to the egg, juice, salt, and pepper in the food processor. Proceed as above.

Tartar Sauce: Prepare Basic Mayonnaise and stir in 1 tablespoon pickle relish and ¼ teaspoon Tabasco sauce.

Wasabi Mayonnaise: Prepare Basic Mayonnaise and stir in 1 to 3 tablespoons wasabi powder (depending on its strength) and 1 teaspoon soy sauce.

Note: Food containing raw eggs should not be served to young children, pregnant women, or anyone in poor health or with a compromised immune system. Buy the freshest eggs possible, and consume the mayonnaise the day you make it.

boiled lobsters with lemon-caper mayonnaise

Lemon-caper mayonnaise *can be stored in the refrigerator for several hours before serving, but is so quick that it can also be made in the food processor while the lobsters are boiling.*

I large egg

2 tablespoons fresh lemon juice

Salt and freshly ground black pepper to taste

I cup neutral-tasting vegetable oil, such as canola

2 tablespoons capers, drained well and coarsely chopped

I teaspoon finely chopped fresh thyme leaves

4 lobsters, I to 1½ pounds each

I. Combine the egg, lemon juice, salt, and pepper in the work bowl of a food processor. Pulse several times to break up the egg. With the motor running, add the vegetable oil in a steady stream and process until the mayonnaise is thick, about I minute. Scrape into a small bowl and stir in the capers and thyme. Season with additional salt and pepper. Refrigerate until serving.

2. Fill a very large pot halfway with water and bring to a boil. Add 2 tablespoons salt and the lobsters. Let the water return to a boil and boil the lobsters until bright red and cooked through, 8 to 10 minutes depending on the size. Remove the lobsters from the water and serve immediately, or cool, refrigerate, and serve cold with the mayonnaise on the side. (See note on page 210.)

makes 4 servings

plain and simple shrimp boil

Additional vegetables *may be added to this boil for variety—two ears of corn cut in half, pearl onions, even artichokes. Season the cooked shrimp with Tabasco, or reserve some of the broth for dipping the shrimp and some crusty bread.*

1 cup fresh lemon juice

1 head garlic, cut in half crosswise

½ cup kosher salt

1 tablespoon cayenne pepper

1 tablespoon sweet paprika

2 teaspoons dried thyme

2 teaspoons ground allspice

2 pounds small red potatoes, scrubbed

2 pounds medium-size shrimp, shells on

Tabasco sauce to taste

1 lemon, cut into 8 wedges

1. Fill a large pot halfway with water. Add the lemon juice, garlic, salt, cayenne, paprika, thyme, and allspice; bring to a boil and boil for 10 minutes. Add the potatoes and boil until almost cooked through, 10 to 15 minutes. Add the shrimp, cover, and remove the pot from the heat. Let stand until shrimp are cooked through, about 5 minutes.

2. Drain and transfer the shrimp and potatoes to a large platter. Serve with cups of broth, Tabasco sauce, and lemon wedges on the side.

makes 4 servings

squid with saffron couscous

This simple mix *of seafood and couscous borrows flavor from traditional paella, but can be put together, start to finish, in half an hour. Buy the smallest squid you can— big ones tend to be tougher. To save yourself time (and if you're at all squeamish about fishy things) buy cleaned squid; frozen is fine if fresh is unavailable. Round out the meal with Blanched Leeks with Ricotta Salata Vinaigrette (page 55) and, for dessert, Rum-Vanilla Panna Cotta (page 234).*

6 tablespoons extra-virgin olive oil

¼ cup fresh lemon juice

1 teaspoon sweet paprika

1 garlic clove, finely chopped

1 pound cleaned squid, cut into
  ¼-inch-thick rings

1½ teaspoons salt

2¼ cups water

¼ teaspoon saffron threads, crushed

One 10-ounce box instant couscous

12 cherry tomatoes, quartered

½ cup green olives, pitted and coarsely
  chopped

2 tablespoons finely chopped fresh parsley
  leaves

1. Combine 5 tablespoons of the olive oil, the lemon juice, paprika, and garlic in a small bowl. Set aside.

2. Bring a large pot of water to boil. Add the squid and 1 teaspoon of the salt and

cook until the squid is opaque, about 30 seconds. Do not overcook or the squid will become rubbery. Drain and pat dry with paper towels.

3. Bring the water and crushed saffron to a boil in a medium-size saucepan. Stir in the couscous, the remaining ½ teaspoon salt, and the remaining tablespoon olive oil. Remove the pan from the heat and cover. Let stand for 5 minutes and fluff with a fork.

4. Transfer the couscous to a large serving bowl. Pour the dressing over the couscous and stir in the squid, tomatoes, olives, and parsley. Serve warm, at room temperature, or chilled.

makes 4 servings

scallops simmered in spiced tomato broth

Sweet, briny scallops *are delicious when simmered in a subtly seasoned broth of tomatoes and spices. Perfect White Rice (page 6) or crusty bread make neutral backgrounds for this tasty dish.*

1 cup canned crushed tomatoes

1 cup water

2 tablespoons extra-virgin olive oil

2 garlic cloves, peeled and crushed

1 jalapeño chile, seeded and finely chopped

4 scallions, white and green parts, finely
   chopped

½ teaspoon ground cumin

½ teaspoon ground coriander

Salt and freshly ground black pepper to taste

1½ pounds sea or bay scallops

1. Combine the tomatoes, water, olive oil, garlic, jalapeño, scallions, cumin, and coriander in a large saucepan and bring to a boil. Reduce the heat to medium-low and simmer for 10 minutes to allow the flavors to meld.

2. Season the broth with salt and pepper. Add the scallops and simmer, stirring once or twice, until they are just opaque, about 4 minutes for bay scallops and 6 minutes for sea scallops. Do not over-cook or the scallops will be tough. Season with salt and pepper again and serve immediately.

makes 4 servings

stovetop sweets

Chilled Strawberry Soup with a Dollop of Yogurt

◆

Brandied Figs over Fresh Ricotta Cheese

◆

Ginger Ice Cream with Warm Apricot Sauce

◆

Peaches in Rosemary–Red Wine Syrup

◆

Oranges in Zesty Syrup

◆

Vanilla Poached Pears with Hazelnut Chocolate Sauce

◆

Fresh Lemon Gelatin and Whipped Cream Parfaits

◆

Rum-Vanilla Panna Cotta

◆

Raspberries in White Zinfandel Jelly

◆

Warm Chocolate-Espresso Pudding

◆

Arborio Rice Pudding

◆

Blueberries with Lemon Pudding

◆

continued

Dark Chocolate–Almond Semifreddo

◆

Maple Mousse

◆

Walnut Praline Candy

Counterintuitive though it may seem, there are, in fact, many beautiful and satisfying desserts that you can prepare if you don't own a cookie sheet and are unfamiliar with the term "preheat." The following recipes require no special equipment or technique. They all satisfy my requirements for both everyday and special-occasion cooking: Each has fresh flavor, is great to look at, and is a snap to prepare.

As a student at culinary school, the very first lessons I learned about dessert making had nothing to do with the oven and everything to do with the stove. Making sugar syrup and caramel, poaching fruit, melting chocolate and gelatin over simmering water—these basics require only a saucepan and a burner. Although I did eventually complete the full course in baking and pastry arts, I now find myself returning over and over again to those earlier techniques. A poached pear drizzled with warm chocolate sauce and garnished with a little chantilly cream has an unfussy beauty. Blush wine jelly layered with fresh raspberries is easy but not at all pedestrian. These desserts complement the simple food I now prepare for my family and friends. They're a

little bit different from a standard piece of pie. And they're a lot easier than pie.

The most basic desserts are made by boiling fruit, sugar, and water to soften, sweeten, and provide a syrup for the fruit. Fruit prepared this way may be flavored and embellished according to taste. Chilled Strawberry Soup has hints of exotic cinnamon, ginger, and star anise. A dollop of yogurt provides a tart counterpoint to the soup's sweetness. Brandied Figs over Fresh Ricotta Cheese, another variation on this theme, has a syrup flavored with brandy and an appropriately rustic garnish of fresh, home-style cheese. Sometimes a syrup is wonderful over uncooked fruit. One satisfyingly minimalist dessert here consists of oranges dressed with their zest, which has been plumped in a simple sugar syrup.

Some of the best no-bake desserts are made with gelatin. Flavorless itself, gelatin transforms a liquid into a semisolid food. Thus, heavy cream heated with some sugar and rum becomes a soothing panna cotta. Lemonade combined with gelatin is spooned into parfait glasses and topped with whipped cream—a refreshing take on a diner classic. There's a reason children have always taken delight in gelatin desserts. Their sparkling appearance and unique texture are *fun.* Although my gelatin recipes contain no artificial coloring or flavoring, no mini marshmallows, and no canned fruit, they do call to mind a simpler culinary past.

Pudding is another stovetop dessert that makes people nostalgic. Like more sophisticated baked custard, flan, and crème brûlée, puddings are wonderfully soothing. But stovetop puddings require no baking, no water baths, no careful measures to prevent curdling. Arborio Rice Pudding flavored with vanilla and enriched with eggs and cream is comfort food beyond compare. For something a little lighter, Blueberries with Lemon Pud-

ding will still satisfy the desire for a silky-smooth dessert. Warm Chocolate–Espresso Pudding is as quick as the "instant" stuff from the supermarket but is made with premium ingredients that give it a deluxe flavor.

I've included two frozen desserts here that are easier and more elegant (always a good combination) than homemade ice cream. Dark Chocolate–Almond Semifreddo is a rich chocolate terrine. This is a great dessert to make for a large dinner party. It is no-bake, do-ahead, and show-stopping. Each slice, studded with almonds and bits of amaretti cookies, is like a super-premium chocolate bar. Maple Mousse is another great do-ahead dinner party dessert, pleasing because of its homey maple flavor and its otherworldly lightness.

Just a few words of advice: A couple of the recipes that follow involve melting chocolate above a pan of barely simmering water. Chocolate is quite an unstable substance, temperamental when it comes to heat. The reason we melt chocolate over indirect heat is to gain control of what happens when it begins to melt. If it comes in direct contact with heat or is heated too quickly over too high a flame, it may separate and become grainy. Since the pleasures of a chocolate dessert include a glossy appearance and smooth texture, we don't want this to happen. When melting chocolate, make sure that the bowl containing the chocolate does not come into direct contact with the water. Also make sure that your water doesn't ever come to a boil. This way, you'll always wind up with velvety melted chocolate.

The last recipe in this chapter is for Walnut Praline Candy—caramel mixed with nuts. Caramel is essentially a matter of just adding water. A little water is combined with some sugar in a heavy pot and the mixture is brought to a boil. Eventually, the water evaporates, the sugar liquefies, and it turns a beautiful amber color. For praline, nuts are stirred into the caramel and the mixture is poured onto a greased pan and allowed to cool and harden into candy. Even though making caramel involves nothing more than boiling sugar and water together until the mixture becomes golden, there are several ways to ruin it.

Stirring after the sugar begins to melt encourages the formation of sugar crystals, which will make your caramel gritty instead of smooth. I never brush the sides of the pot with a damp pastry brush, as many people suggest, because this may possibly encourage crystal formation even though it's supposed to dissolve crystals. So resist the urge to stir or fuss with the sugar-water mixture in any way. Just pour the sugar and water in the pan, tilt to moisten the sugar, and turn on the heat.

Once the sugar has dissolved, keep a careful watch. If you notice that the sugar syrup is browning in one spot more quickly than in others, gently tilt the pan to distribute the heat. Remove the pan from the heat as soon as the syrup is light amber. It will continue to cook quickly while it's in the hot pot, so you want to take it off the heat a few seconds before it looks dark enough. And beware: Sugar cooks at a very high temperature and hot caramel is *very* hot. For safety's sake, be sure to use very well-insulated oven mitts when handling the pot.

The transformation of granulated sugar into caramel is one of the most amazing kitchen tricks that I know. Don't lose heart if you burn your first batch. Just fill the pot with water, bring it to a boil to dissolve the burnt sugar, and start again.

chilled strawberry soup with a dollop of yogurt

Yogurt is *a delicious, low-fat garnish for this light dessert soup, but sour cream, whipped cream, or vanilla ice cream would also work well.*

2 pints fresh strawberries, hulled and halved

2 cups orange juice

½ cup sugar

1 cinnamon stick

One 1-inch piece fresh gingerroot, peeled

1 dried star anise (optional)

1 cup plain low-fat yogurt

1. Combine 1½ pints of the strawberries, the orange juice, sugar, cinnamon stick, ginger, and star anise in a medium-size saucepan. Bring to a boil. Reduce the heat to medium-low and simmer until the berries have almost disintegrated, about 15 minutes.

2. Remove the cinnamon stick, ginger, and star anise. Carefully pour the hot mixture into a blender or food processor and process until smooth. Transfer to a bowl and stir in the remaining ½ pint strawberries. Refrigerate until chilled, 1 to 1½ hours. Ladle the soup into four bowls and garnish each with ¼ cup of the yogurt.

makes 4 servings

brandied figs over fresh ricotta cheese

Fresh figs *are rarely available where I live. So I often plump up dried figs in water and brandy and serve them over ricotta cheese when I want a rustic but sophisticated winter dessert. The best ricotta cheese comes from Italian delis where it is made fresh daily.*

12 dried figs, tough stems removed

1 cup water

1 cup brandy

¼ cup sugar

1½ cups fresh ricotta cheese

1. Combine the figs, water, brandy, and sugar in a medium-size saucepan and bring to a boil. Reduce the heat to medium-low and simmer, stirring frequently, until the liquid is slightly thickened and syrupy and the fruit is softened but still holding its shape, 20 to 25 minutes. Remove from the heat and cool to room temperature. You can refrigerate the figs and syrup for up to 5 days. Bring to room temperature before serving.

2. Cut each fig in half. Divide the ricotta among four dessert bowls and spoon the figs and some syrup over the cheese. Serve immediately.

makes 4 servings

ginger ice cream with warm apricot sauce

Spicy ginger *and syrupy apricots contrast well in this dessert. The combination is so flavorful that I often use low-fat ice cream and don't miss the calories at all. Small plums can be prepared the same way if apricots are not available. Crystallized ginger is available in the spice section of the supermarket.*

I pint vanilla ice cream

¼ cup finely chopped crystallized ginger

6 apricots (about ¾ pound), quartered and pitted

½ cup water

¼ cup sugar

¼ teaspoon ground cinnamon

I. Let the ice cream stand at room temperature until it is softened, but not melted, about 15 minutes. Turn it into a bowl, add the ginger, and quickly mix with the back of a large spoon to incorporate the ginger. Cover the bowl with plastic wrap and return the ice cream to the freezer.

2. Combine the apricots, water, sugar, and cinnamon in a medium-size saucepan. Bring to a boil, reduce the heat to medium-low, and simmer until the fruit has become very soft but has not entirely disintegrated, 10 to 12 minutes. Remove from the heat and let stand until it is warm, not hot, to the touch, 8 to 10 minutes.

3. Divide the ice cream among four dessert bowls. Spoon the warm apricot sauce over the ice cream and serve immediately.

makes 4 servings

peaches in rosemary—
red wine syrup

This is a dessert *for grown-ups, sweet but subtle. If you're a real sophisticate, set a chunk of Reggiano-Parmigiano on the table for nibbling along with the wine-soaked fruit.*

I cup Chianti or other dry red wine

I cup water

½ cup sugar

One 3-inch-long sprig fresh rosemary

8 firm but ripe peaches, pitted and cut into
quarters

I. Combine the wine, water, and sugar in a small saucepan and bring to a boil over medium-high heat. Reduce the heat to low and simmer until the mixture is reduced by half, 8 to 10 minutes. Pour the syrup into a heatproof bowl or measuring cup. Add the rosemary and steep for 5 minutes. Remove the rosemary, cool the syrup to room temperature, and then refrigerate until cold, about I hour, or up to 3 days.

2. Divide the sliced peaches among four dessert bowls. Pour the syrup over the fruit and serve.

makes 4 servings

oranges in zesty syrup

Here's a *refreshing way to end a winter meal. The cooked zest lends zingy tartness to the sweetened oranges. Serve the oranges on their own or garnished with a small scoop of vanilla ice cream or a sprig of mint.*

4 navel oranges

¾ cup sugar

6 tablespoons water

2 tablespoons Grand Marnier or other
   orange liqueur

Vanilla ice cream (optional)

Fresh mint leaves (optional)

1. Remove the zest from the oranges with a vegetable peeler, leaving behind the white pith. With a sharp paring knife, cut the zest into long, thin strips. Place the zest in a small saucepan, cover with water, and bring to a boil. Reduce the heat to medium-low and simmer for 1 minute. Drain the zest and plunge it into a bowl of cold water. Set aside.

2. Combine the sugar and water in another small saucepan and bring to a boil, stirring occasionally to dissolve the sugar. Reduce the heat to medium-low and simmer for 10 minutes. Drain the zest and add it to the syrup. Simmer until the zest softens slightly, another 2 minutes. Remove from the heat and stir in the liqueur.

3. Using a sharp paring knife and your fingers, remove any remaining white pith from the oranges. With a sharp knife (I

use a serrated tomato knife), slice each orange into ½-inch-thick rounds, cutting from blossom end to stem end. Place the orange slices in an airtight container and pour the syrup and zest over them. Refrigerate until well chilled, 2 to 3 hours. To serve, place several slices of orange in each of four dessert bowls and spoon some syrup and zest over each serving. Garnish with a small scoop of vanilla ice cream or some mint leaves if desired.

makes 4 servings

vanilla poached pears with hazelnut chocolate sauce

This classic dessert *requires two pots of simmering water—one for the pears and one for the chocolate sauce. The only thing new or strange here is the way the pears are positioned in the pot. A circle of parchment paper is placed on the cut surface of the pears after they are placed in the water to prevent any browning that might occur because of exposure to the air. Cooking parchment is available at supermarkets and houseware stores.*

FOR THE PEARS

6 cups cold water

1 cup sugar

2 tablespoons fresh lemon juice

4 ripe pears (1½ to 2 pounds)

½ split vanilla bean

FOR THE CHOCOLATE SAUCE

4 ounces bittersweet chocolate, chopped

¼ cup water

1 tablespoon hazelnut liqueur

FOR THE WHIPPED CREAM

½ cup heavy cream

1 tablespoon sugar

1. Make the pears. Cut a piece of parchment paper into a circle the same size as the large, wide saucepan you'll be using

to poach the pears. Combine the water, I cup sugar, and the lemon juice in the saucepan. Peel the pears, halve them lengthwise, and carefully scoop out the core with a teaspoon or melon baller. After you peel, halve, and core each pear, immediately place it in the water-and-lemon mixture cut side up. When all the pears are in the water, add the vanilla bean and place the parchment circle on top of the pears. Lightly press down to make sure that the pears are submerged in the water. Bring to a boil, then reduce the heat to medium-low and simmer for 2 minutes. Turn off the heat and let the pears cool in the liquid, about I hour. Watch the pot carefully and do not overcook or you'll get mushy pears. Place the pears and the liquid in an airtight container and refrigerate until ready to use. The poached pears may be refrigerated up to 2 days.

2. Make the chocolate sauce. Put 2 inches of water in a medium-size saucepan and bring to a bare simmer. Combine the chocolate and water in a stainless steel bowl big enough to rest on top of the saucepan and place it on top of the simmering water, making sure that the water doesn't touch the bowl. Heat, whisking occasionally, until the chocolate is completely melted. Turn off the heat. Stir in the liqueur. The sauce may be refrigerated for up to 2 days. Reheat in the microwave for I½ minutes or over a pot of simmering water.

3. Make the cream. Whip the heavy cream and the tablespoon of sugar together with an electric mixer until it holds soft peaks.

4. Drain the pears and pat them dry with a clean dish towel. Cut each half into thin slices, leaving the slices attached to each other at the stem end. Fan two pear halves on each of four dessert plates. Drizzle with the chocolate sauce and place a dollop of the whipped cream on each plate. Serve immediately.

makes 4 servings

poaching fruit

Poaching is an especially handy technique for improving on fruit that is not at peak ripeness or may be lacking in flavor. Poached fruit is soft but retains its shape. It absorbs the sweetness and flavor of the liquid it is cooked in. Serve poached fruit with whipped cream, crème fraîche, mascarpone, ricotta, or ice cream, or serve with a plate of crisp cookies for some textural contrast. Two pounds of the following fruit can be poached in 6 cups water, 1 cup sugar, 2 tablespoons fresh lemon juice, and ½ split vanilla bean. Alternatively, the same amount of fruit (except the pineapple) can be poached in 3 cups red wine, 3 cups water, 1 cup sugar, 1 cinnamon stick, and 1 long strip of lemon zest.

Apricots: Use ripe but firm fruit. Halve and pit the apricots. Place in a heatproof bowl. Bring the syrup ingredients to a boil and pour over the apricots. Let stand for 5 minutes, then add 6 to 8 ice cubes to stop the cooking. Refrigerate the fruit in the syrup until ready to use, up to 2 days.

Cherries: Pit the cherries. Place in a heatproof bowl. Bring the syrup ingredients to a boil and pour over the cherries. Let stand for 5 minutes, then add 6 to 8 ice cubes to stop the cooking. Refrigerate the fruit in the syrup until ready to use, up to 2 days.

Nectarines and peaches: Use ripe but firm fruit. Peel with a vegetable peeler, halve, and pit. Cover the fruit and liquid with a circle of parchment paper, as in the recipe for poached pears. Bring the fruit and liquid to a boil, reduce the heat to medium-low, and cook at a bare simmer until the fruit is tender when pierced with a paring knife, 3 to 5 minutes. Immediately remove the fruit from the hot liquid with a slotted spoon and cool on a plate lined with a clean dish towel to absorb excess liquid. If the fruit isn't to be used immediately, cool the syrup, return the fruit to the syrup, and refrigerate until ready to use, up to 2 days.

Pineapple: Peel and quarter the pineapple. Cut away the core from each quarter and cut each quarter into ¼-inch-thick slices. Cover the fruit and liquid with a circle of parchment paper, as in the recipe for poached pears. Bring the fruit and syrup to a boil, reduce the heat to medium-low, and cook at a bare simmer until the fruit is tender when pierced with a paring knife, 5 to 7 minutes. Cool the fruit in the syrup. Refrigerate the fruit in the syrup until ready to use, up to 2 days.

Plums: Use ripe but firm fruit. Halve and pit the plums. Place in a heatproof bowl. Bring the syrup ingredients to a boil and pour over the plums. Let stand for 5 minutes, then add 6 to 8 ice cubes to stop the cooking. Refrigerate the fruit in the syrup until ready to use, up to 2 days.

Prunes: Use 1, not 2, pounds fruit. Bring the fruit and poaching liquid to a boil, reduce the heat to medium-low, and cook at a bare simmer until the prunes are tender, 20 to 30 minutes. Cool the prunes in the syrup. Refrigerate the fruit in the syrup until ready to use, up to 5 days.

fresh lemon gelatin and whipped cream parfaits

With all the hoopla *surrounding the one hundredth anniversary of Jell-O (including a front-page* New York Times *story), many pastry chefs are rethinking gelatin desserts. Suddenly, they can be found on the menus of the best restaurants in town. Here's my contribution: Lemon gelatin, made with fresh lemon juice, tastes immeasurably better than its commercial counterpart but shares the same sparkling appearance. Rich whipped cream complements the light texture and flavor of the jelly.*

2 envelopes unflavored gelatin

2½ cups cold water

1 cup plus 2 tablespoons sugar

1 cup fresh lemon juice

½ teaspoon grated lemon zest

½ cup heavy cream

4 sprigs fresh mint (optional)

I. In a small bowl, sprinkle the gelatin over ½ cup of the cold water and let soften for 2 minutes. Combine the remaining 2 cups water, 1 cup of the sugar, and the lemon juice and zest in a medium-size saucepan and bring to a boil. Turn the heat off and whisk in the gelatin mixture. Whisk for 1 minute to dissolve any lumps. Pour into a bowl and refrigerate until firm, at least 6 hours and up to 1 day.

2. Combine the heavy cream and the remaining 2 tablespoons sugar in a medium-size bowl and whip with an electric mixer until the cream holds soft peaks. Spoon one-eighth of the jelly into each of four goblets or sundae glasses. Top with one-eighth of the whipped cream. Divide the remaining jelly among the four goblets and top with the remaining whipped cream. Garnish with fresh mint leaves, if desired.

makes 4 servings

rum-vanilla panna cotta

Rum gives this *traditional Italian gelatin dessert a little bit of an edge and keeps it from becoming rubbery in the style of commercial gelatin. The vanilla bean gives each pudding a pretty speckled top. Serve with fresh fruit scattered around each individual serving. Tropical fruits like mango or papaya work well with the rum and vanilla flavors of the pudding, but raspberries, strawberries, peaches, and nectarines are good, too.*

½ cup milk

I envelope unflavored gelatin

2 cups heavy cream

½ cup sugar

¼ cup dark rum

½ vanilla bean, split

3 cups fresh fruit (raspberries, sliced strawberries, sliced mango, and sliced peaches are all good)

I. Pour the milk into a small bowl and sprinkle with the gelatin; let stand until the gelatin dissolves, I to 2 minutes.

2. Combine the heavy cream, sugar, rum, and vanilla bean in a medium-size saucepan and bring to a boil. Remove from the heat, add the gelatin mixture, and whisk constantly for I minute to dissolve the gelatin. Remove and discard the vanilla bean and pour the panna cotta into four ramekins or custard cups. Refrigerate until firm, at least 6 hours or overnight.

3. To unmold the panna cottas, fill a medium-size bowl with very hot tap water. One at a time, run a paring knife around each panna cotta to separate it from the sides of the ramekin and then dip the bottom half of the ramekin in the water for 30 seconds. Place a small dessert plate on top of the mold, invert, tap the bottom of the mold, and lift the mold off the plate. Arrange some fruit around each panna cotta and serve immediately.

makes 4 servings

raspberries in white zinfandel jelly

This recipe *was conceived out of the desperation to do something with a bottle of wine that nobody in my house actually wanted to drink. While I find white zinfandel too cloying with most food, I love the way it is transformed into a not-too-sweet dessert. As a bonus, the pale pink jelly and the bright red raspberries are strikingly pretty.*

1 envelope unflavored gelatin

¾ cup cold water

½ cup plus 1 tablespoon sugar

3 cups white zinfandel or other fruity rosé wine

1 pint fresh raspberries

1. In a small bowl, sprinkle the gelatin over the water and let soften for 2 minutes. Combine ½ cup of the sugar and the wine in a medium-size sauce pan and bring to a boil. Turn the heat off and whisk in the gelatin mixture. Whisk for 1 minute to dissolve any lumps. Pour into a bowl and refrigerate until firm, at least 6 hours and up to 1 day.

2. Combine the berries and the remaining tablespoon sugar in a small bowl and let stand, stirring once or twice, until the sugar dissolves, about 20 minutes. Spoon a few raspberries into the bottom of each of four goblets or sundae glasses. Spoon half the jelly into the glasses. Top with half the remaining raspberries. Divide the remaining jelly among the four goblets and top with the remaining raspberries. Serve immediately.

makes 4 servings

warm chocolate-espresso pudding

This deep, *dark pudding is rich and satisfying enough to serve to dinner guests, but quick and simple enough to make on the spur of the moment when you're craving something warm and chocolate.*

¼ **cup cornstarch**

6 **tablespoons sugar**

I **tablespoon plus I teaspoon instant espresso**

I¼ **cups heavy cream**

I¼ **cups milk**

6 **ounces bittersweet chocolate, finely chopped**

I **tablespoon unsalted butter**

I. Combine the cornstarch, sugar, and espresso powder in a medium-size saucepan. Whisk in ½ cup of the heavy cream until the mixture is smooth.

2. Add the remaining ¾ cup heavy cream and the milk and bring to a boil, whisking constantly. Continue to cook over medium-high heat, whisking, until the mixture thickens, 3 to 4 minutes.

3. Remove from the heat and whisk in the chocolate and butter, continuing to whisk until all the chocolate and butter have melted and the pudding is very smooth. Spoon into four dessert goblets and serve warm or refrigerate up to 24 hours and serve cold.

makes 4 servings

arborio rice pudding

Arborio rice, *imported from Italy, makes the creamiest, most luxurious rice pudding. It is available in most supermarkets and Italian delis.*

1 cup Arborio rice

5 cups milk

¾ cup sugar

½ vanilla bean, split lengthwise

1 cup heavy cream

2 large eggs

½ cup dark or golden raisins

¼ teaspoon ground cinnamon

1. Combine the rice, milk, sugar, and vanilla bean in a large saucepan and bring to a boil. Reduce the heat to medium-low and simmer, uncovered, until the rice is tender and most of the milk is absorbed, 35 to 40 minutes.

2. Bring the heavy cream to a boil in a small saucepan. Whisk the eggs together in a medium-size bowl to break them up. Very slowly whisk the boiling milk into the eggs (don't add the milk all at once or the eggs will cook and curdle). Stir the egg mixture into the pot of rice and simmer, stirring occasionally, until it begins to thicken, 3 to 4 minutes. Remove from the heat and stir in the raisins and cinnamon. Cool slightly, remove the vanilla bean, and serve warm, or transfer to a bowl, place plastic wrap directly on the surface, refrigerate at least 2 hours or overnight, and serve cold.

makes 6 servings

blueberries with lemon pudding

This lemon pudding *is less tricky than traditional lemon curd because it relies on cornstarch, rather than the precise cooking of egg yolks, to thicken it. It's also nice and light because it contains no milk or heavy cream. If you like something crunchy to accompany your pudding, stick two store-bought Italian ladyfinger cookies into each goblet before serving.*

1¼ cups water

½ cup sugar

Pinch of salt

2 large eggs, lightly beaten

2 tablespoons cornstarch

¼ cup fresh lemon juice

1 teaspoon grated lemon zest

1 pint fresh blueberries, picked over and washed

8 ladyfingers (optional)

1. Combine 1 cup of the water, the sugar, salt, and eggs in a medium-size saucepan. Whisk together the cornstarch and the remaining ¼ cup water in a small bowl and add it to the saucepan. Over low heat, whisk constantly until the sugar is dissolved and the mixture begins to thicken, about 10 minutes. Pour into a nonreactive container and stir in the lemon juice and zest. Cool to room temperature and refrigerate until chilled, at least 1 hour.

2. Divide the blueberries among four dessert bowls or goblets. Spoon the lemon pudding over each serving. Garnish with ladyfingers, if desired.

makes 4 servings

dark chocolate–almond semifreddo

This is a simple *but incredibly rich special-occasion dessert. If you use high-quality chocolate (I like Lindt or Ghirardelli, two brands my supermarket carries), each slice tastes like a super-premium chocolate bar. Serve with sweetened, softly whipped cream.*

16 ounces bittersweet chocolate, finely chopped

3 tablespoons unsalted butter

6 large egg yolks

6 tablespoons sugar

1 cup coarsely chopped amaretti cookies

1 cup coarsely chopped almonds

2 tablespoons Amaretto or other almond liqueur

2 teaspoons pure vanilla extract

1 cup heavy cream, plus extra for garnish

1. Line a 9½ × 4 × 3-inch loaf pan with plastic wrap, making sure that the wrap is tucked into all the corners and that there is at least 1 inch overhanging the top of the pan on all sides.

2. Put 2 inches of water in a medium-size saucepan and bring to a bare simmer. Combine the chocolate and butter in a stainless steel bowl big enough to rest on top of the saucepan and place it on top of the simmering water, making sure that the bowl doesn't touch the water. Heat, whisking occasionally, until the chocolate and butter are completely

melted. Remove from the heat and set aside.

3. Whisk the egg yolks and ¼ cup of the sugar together in another stainless steel bowl and place the bowl over the still-simmering water. Whisk constantly until the sugar has dissolved (you won't be able to feel any grittiness when you stick your finger in the bowl) and the mixture is warm but not hot, 6 to 8 minutes. Remove from the heat and slowly whisk in the chocolate mixture. Stir in the cookies, almonds, liqueur, and vanilla.

4. Whip 1 cup of the heavy cream with the remaining 2 tablespoons sugar with an electric mixer until soft peaks form. In three separate additions, gently fold the whipped cream into the chocolate mixture, being careful not to deflate the cream. Gently scrape the semifreddo into the loaf pan and smooth the top with a spatula. Cover the top with plastic and refrigerate until firm, at least 6 hours and up to 1 day.

5. To unmold, gently tug the plastic wrap that lines the pan to loosen the semifreddo. Place a large plate over the pan and turn it over. Gently tap to release the semifreddo. Peel the plastic wrap from the semifreddo and cut into slices with a sharp knife. Garnish with additional whipped cream if desired.

makes 10 to 12 servings

Note: Raw eggs should not be used in food to be consumed by children, pregnant women, or anyone in poor health or with a compromised immune system. Make sure you buy the freshest eggs possible.

maple mousse

This frozen dessert *has a nice, strong maple flavor but is lighter and more delicate in texture than ice cream. An optional sprinkle of walnut praline adds some crunch. Homemade gingersnaps would also make an excellent accompaniment.*

4 large egg yolks

½ cup pure maple syrup

2 tablespoons dark rum

1⅓ cups heavy cream

Walnut Praline Candy (optional; page 244), ground in a food processor

1. Put 2 inches of water into a small saucepan and bring to a bare simmer. Combine the yolks and maple syrup in a stainless steel bowl and place it on top of the simmering water, making sure that the bowl doesn't touch the water. Heat, whisking constantly, until slightly thickened and lighter in color, 6 to 8 min-utes. Remove from the heat and whip with the whisk attachment of an electric mixer until completely cool, 7 to 10 minutes. Stir in the rum.

2. Whip the heavy cream with an electric mixer until soft peaks form. In three separate additions, gently fold the whipped cream into the maple mixture, being careful not to deflate the cream. Spoon the semifreddo into four large dessert goblets and freeze until firm, at least 2 hours and up to 1 day. If desired, sprinkle some praline on top of the mousse immediately before serving.

makes 4 servings

Note: Raw eggs should not be used in food to be consumed by children, pregnant women, or anyone in poor health or with a compromised immune system. Make sure you buy the freshest eggs possible.

walnut praline candy

Making praline *or any other kind of hard caramel is as easy as boiling water, as long as you remember one thing—*don't stir! *Stirring encourages sugar crystals to form on the side of the pan, preventing your caramel from becoming smooth. Just pour the sugar and water into the pan, tilt it a little to moisten the sugar, and let it sit on top of the flame. One more thing—watch carefully. There are only a few seconds between perfect caramel and burnt sugar. As soon as your sugar has turned a light amber color, stir in the nuts (pecans, almonds, hazelnuts, peanuts, or even pine nuts may be substituted) and pour into a greased pan. Work quickly, before the candy hardens. To clean up the pan, fill it with water and bring to a boil to dissolve the sugar stuck to the bottom and sides.*

1 cup sugar

¼ cup water

1¼ cups walnut halves, coarsely chopped

1. Line an 8-inch square baking pan with aluminum foil and grease the foil with butter. Grease a wooden spoon and a metal spatula with butter also. Combine the sugar and water in a small saucepan.

Bring to a boil and cook until the mixture turns a light amber color. Do not stir. If parts of the syrup are turning darker than others, gently tilt the pan to even out the cooking.

2. As soon as the syrup is a uniformly amber color, stir in the nuts with the greased spoon. Pour the mixture into the prepared pan and smooth with the but-

tered spatula. Work quickly because the praline will begin to harden soon after it is removed from the heat. Allow the mixture to cool completely. When hardened, turn the praline out of the pan and chop into small chunks with a chef's knife. Or place in the work bowl of a food proces-

sor and pulse several times to finely chop. Praline will keep at room temperature in an airtight container for several weeks.

makes about ¾ pound

how to boil a dinner party

If you know nothing except how to boil water, you are not a cooking idiot. Get out a saucepan, and you are well on your way to a fabulous dinner of Asian-Style Stewed Pork with Water Chestnuts and Snow Peas (page 186), Perfect White Rice (page 6), Blanched Spinach with Sesame–Rice Wine Vinegar Dressing (page 56), and Ginger Ice Cream with Warm Apricot Sauce (page 224).

Think about it: For the pork, you throw some cubed meat, water, soy sauce, chiles, garlic, and vegetables into a pot and turn on the stove. The spinach is just dumped in salted boiling water for a few minutes, drained in a colander, and then tossed with a simple but flavorful salad dressing. For dessert, mix a little chopped crystallized ginger with store-bought vanilla ice cream and serve with a sauce of apricots that have been peeled, pitted, and cooked in a little water with some sugar and spices.

Here are some more menus, to give you an idea of how simple and interesting it is to put together a complete meal by just adding water:

best boiled brunch
Grits and Goat Cheese (page 30)
Spinach Salad with Ham and Poached Eggs (page 35)
Dried Fruit Compote (page 39)

seafood supper with spanish flavors
Blanched Asparagus with Olive Oil and Manchego Cheese (page 45)
Squid with Saffron Couscous (page 213)
Oranges in Zesty Syrup (page 226)

weeknight dinner with asian favors

Clams in Thai-Seasoned Broth (page 203)

Coconut Rice with Scallions and Peanuts
(page 139)

Sliced fresh mango and pineapple

simple, satisfying pasta dinner

Spaghetti alla Carbonara (page 132)

Green salad

Peaches in Rosemary–Red Wine Syrup
(page 225)

fresh, light vegetarian dinner

Pearl Barley and Pesto (page 151)

Sliced tomatoes

Chilled Strawberry Soup with a Dollop of
Yogurt (page 222)

luxurious late night supper

Boiled Arborio Rice with Smoked Salmon and
Capers (page 145)

Arugula dressed with olive oil and lemon juice

Warm Chocolate-Espresso Pudding
(page 237)

down-home sunday supper

Red Beans, Sausages, and Rice (page 180)

Boiled okra or green beans

Fresh Lemon Gelatin and Whipped Cream
Parfaits (page 232)

best blue-plate special dinner

Corned Beef and Cabbage (page 168)

Arborio Rice Pudding (page 238)

weeknight dinner with spice

Polenta with Fresh Corn and Chives
(page 147)

Braised Pork with Chipotle Chiles (page 178)

Green salad

Fruit sorbet with fresh berries

chilled celebration for spring or summer

Cold Poached Salmon with Tomato-Mint
Salsa (page 195)

Rice Salad with Cucumber and Dill
(page 140)

Raspberries in White Zinfandel Jelly
(page 236)

casual but stylish seafood dinner

White Beans with Shrimp (page 112)

Cod Fillets in Fennel Broth (page 199)

Maple Mousse (page 242)

exotic vegetarian flavors

Couscous with Black Olives and Orange Zest
 (page 138)

Blanched Cauliflower with Charmoula
 (page 50)

Blanched Leeks with Ricotta Salata Vinaigrette
 (page 55)

Peppermint Hot Chocolate (page 27)

classic shrimp boil with trimmings

Plain and Simple Shrimp Boil (page 212)

Corn on the cob

Green salad

Blueberries with Lemon Pudding (page 239)

country-french comfort food

Hearty Beef Stew (page 165)

White Bean Puree (page 106)

Green salad

Vanilla Poached Pears with Hazelnut Chocolate Sauce (page 228)

country-italian feast

Italian Tomato and Bread Soup (page 76)

Boiled Beef with Salsa Verde (page 166)

Broccoli Rabe with Garlic-Chile Oil
 (page 48)

Parmesan and Basil Mashed Potatoes
 (page 63)

Brandied Figs over Fresh Ricotta Cheese
 (page 223)

latin american fantasy

Lentils in Habanero Oil (page 95)

Braised Pork Roast with Yams (page 176)

Perfect White Rice (page 6)

Rum-Vanilla Panna Cotta (page 234)

Index

chive(s) (*continued*)
    and dill mashed potatoes, 63
    polenta with fresh corn and, 147
chocolate:
    cream, French roast coffee with, 26
    dark, –almond semifreddo, 240–241
    -espresso pudding, warm, 237
    hazelnut sauce, vanilla poached pears with, 228–229
    hot peppermint, 27
    melting of, 16, 220–221
    white, sauce, 17
chopped spiced zucchini and olives, 57
chowder, Manhattan clam, 77–78
cider syrup, apple, 15
cilantro, Mexican red beans with chipotle chiles and, 104–105
clam(s):
    Manhattan chowder, 77–78
    and spaghetti in hearty tomato sauce, 201–202
    steamer, 13
    steaming tips for, 12
    in Thai-seasoned broth, 203–204
coconut rice with scallions and peanuts, 139
cod fillets in fennel broth, 199–200
coffee, French roast, with chocolate cream, 26
colanders, 18
cooking methods:
    blanching, 43
    boiling, 5
    with double boilers, 16
    poaching, 9
    reducing, 14
    simmering, 7
    steaming, 12
coriander-cumin dressing, bulgur and carrots with, 154–155
corn, fresh, polenta with chives and, 147
corned beef and cabbage, 168–169
couscous, 125–126

with black olives and orange zest, 138
with dried apricots and pistachios, 137
honey-date breakfast, 32
Moroccan-flavored chicken and, 193–194
saffron, squid with, 213–214
crab, steaming tips for, 12
cream:
    of carrot soup, curried, 73
    chocolate, French roast coffee with, 26
    whipped, and fresh lemon gelatin parfaits, 232–233
cucumber, rice salad with dill and, 140
cumin and chickpea dip, 109
cumin-coriander dressing, bulgur and carrots with, 154–155
curried:
    chicken salad with mango, 187
    cream of carrot soup, 73
    mayonnaise, 210
    yogurt, spiced chickpeas and spinach with, 118–119

date-honey breakfast couscous, 32
desserts, *see* sweets
dill:
    and chive mashed potatoes, 63
    -lemon pesto, new potatoes with, 59
    rice salad with cucumber and, 140
dinners, 158–214
    Asian-style stewed pork with water chestnuts and snow peas, 179–180
    beef short ribs with exotic spices, 170–171
    beer-braised short ribs, 172–173
    blanquette of veal, 174–175
    boiled beef with salsa verde, 166–167
    boiled lobsters with lemon-caper mayonnaise, 211
    braised pork roast with yams, 176
    braised pork with chipotle chiles, 178
    chicken and rice, 191–192
    chicken breasts poached in wild mushroom broth, 189–190

French potato salad with tarragon and chives, 58
French roast coffee with chocolate cream, 26
fruit:
    dried, compote, 39
    poaching of, 230–231
    see also specific fruits
fusilli, 126
fusilli with raw tomato-avocado sauce, 128

garlic:
    -chile oil, broccoli rabe with, 48
    mashed potatoes, 62
    mayonnaise, 209
    —red pepper mayonnaise, 210
gelatin, fresh lemon, and whipped cream parfaits,
        232–233
ginger:
    hot lemonade, 25
    ice cream with warm apricot sauce, 224
    vinaigrette, chicken salad with grapefruit and,
        188
goat cheese and carrot puree, 67
goat cheese and grits, 30
Gorgonzola mashed potatoes, 62
grains, 120–157
    pasta, *see* pasta
    simmering of, 7
    types of, 125–127
    see also specific grains
granola, 29
grapefruit, chicken salad with ginger vinaigrette and,
        188
gravy skimmers, 18
grits and goat cheese, 30

habanero oil, lentils in, 95
ham:
    in main-course salads, 142
    spinach salad with poached eggs and, 35–36

and warm potato salad, salmon poached in white
        wine over, 197–198
hazelnut chocolate sauce, vanilla poached pears with,
        228–229
herbs:
    chicken and herbed dumpling soup, 81–82
    green bean salad with yogurt and, 52
    lima beans with butter and, 115
    see also specific herbs
hollandaise sauce, classic, 38
honey-date breakfast couscous, 32
horseradish, sour cream mashed potatoes and leeks
        with, 62
huevos rancheros, 37
hummus, 108

ice cream, ginger, with warm apricot sauce, 224
Indonesian peanut sauce, egg noodles with, 129
Italian style:
    orzo with prosciutto and peas, 136
    pasta e fagioli, 114
    rum-vanilla panna cotta, 234–235
    spaghetti alla carbonara, 132–133
    stewed green beans, 53
    stracciatella, 83
    tomato and bread soup, 76

jelly, white zinfandel, raspberries in, 236

kohlrabi, boiled, with butter and bread crumbs, 54

leeks, blanched, with ricotta salata vinaigrette, 55
leeks and sour cream mashed potatoes with horseradish,
        62
lemon:
    avgolemono, 84
    boiled Arborio rice with Parmesan and, 144
    -caper mayonnaise, boiled lobster with, 211
    -dill pesto, new potatoes with, 59

sweet sauces (*continued*)

    warm apricot, ginger ice cream with, 224

    white chocolate, 17

Swiss chard, polenta with simmered tomato sauce and, 148–149

syrups:

    apple cider, 15

    rosemary–red wine, peaches in, 225

    zesty, oranges in, 226–227

tarragon:

    classic French potato salad with chives and, 58

    vinaigrette, cannellini and green bean salad with, 110–111

    -walnut quinoa, 156

tartar sauce, 210

Thai-seasoned broth, clams in, 203–204

tomato(es):

    and bread soup, Italian, 76

    hearty sauce, spaghetti and clams in, 201–202

    and lentil soup, simplest spicy, 94

    -mint salsa, cold poached salmon with, 195–196

    raw, -avocado sauce, fusilli with, 128

    simmered sauce, polenta with Swiss chard and, 148–149

    spiced broth, scallops simmered in, 215

    sun-dried, and chickpea dip, 109

    sun-dried, blanched broccoli with lemon dressing and, 46

turkey, in main-course salads, 142

vanilla poached pears with hazelnut chocolate sauce, 228–229

vanilla-rum panna cotta, 234–235

veal, blanquette of, 174–175

vegetable(s), 40–67

    bitter, 43

    blanching of, 43

    boiling tips for, 5

chicken soup, 85

    purees of, 43–44, 71

    steaming tips for, 12

    winter, puree, 66

    see also specific vegetables

vinaigrettes:

    ginger, chicken salad with grapefruit and, 188

    ricotta salata, blanched leeks with, 55

    sherry, chicken and orange salad with, 188

    tarragon, cannellini and green bean salad with, 110–111

walnut:

    dressing, kidney beans with, 102–103

    praline candy, 244–245

    -tarragon quinoa, 156

wasabi mayonnaise, 210

water chestnuts, Asian-style stewed pork with snow peas and, 179–180

watercress and fava bean soup, 116

white chocolate sauce, 17

white rice, perfect, 6

wine:

    raspberries in white zinfandel jelly, 236

    red,–rosemary syrup, peaches in, 225

    white, mussels in, over spaghetti, 207–208

    white, salmon poached in, over warm potato and ham salad, 197–198

winter vegetable puree, 66

wire whisks, 19

wooden spoons, 19

yams, braised pork roast with, 176–177

yogurt:

    chilled strawberry soup with a dollop of, 222

    curried, spiced chickpeas and spinach with, 118–119

    green bean salad with herbs and, 52

zinfandel, white, raspberries in jelly of, 236

zucchini, chopped spiced olives and, 57

8/5/99

DATE DUE

OC 2 2 '99			

Demco, Inc. 38-293